BRITAIN'S
SLAVE
EMPIRE

BRITAIN'S SLAVE EMPIRE

James Walvin

TEMPUS

First published 2000

PUBLISHED IN THE UNITED KINGDOM BY:

Tempus Publishing Ltd
The Mill, Brimscombe Port
Stroud, Gloucestershire GL5 2QG

PUBLISHED IN THE UNITED STATES OF AMERICA BY:

Tempus Publishing Inc.
2A Cumberland Street
Charleston, SC 29401

Tempus books are available in France, Germany and Belgium
from the following addresses:

Tempus Publishing Group	Tempus Publishing Group	Tempus Publishing Group
21 Avenue de la République	Gustav-Adolf-Straße 3	Place de L'Alma 4/5
37300 Joué-lès-Tours	99084 Erfurt	1200 Brussels
FRANCE	GERMANY	BELGIUM

British Library Cataloguing in Publication Data.
A catalogue record for this book is available from the British Library.

ISBN 0 7524 1779 7

Typesetting and origination by Tempus Publishing.
PRINTED AND BOUND IN GREAT BRITAIN.

Contents

Introduction

African slaves and their local-born descendants were key elements in the human and economic transformation of large parts of the Americas. Brazil, the Caribbean and parts of North America imported millions of Africans from the Atlantic slave ships in their endeavours to bring local agricultural settlements to profitable development, mainly through the cultivation of tropical staples (sugar, tobacco, rice, cotton and a number of other commodities). Africans were the key human tool used by Europeans in the creation and development of a number of their new empires across the Americas. In this long and complex process, the British played a central role.

Though not the initiators or pioneers of Atlantic slavery, the British perfected it and honed it to a remarkable degree of commercial and maritime success. Two regions of the Americas – the British West Indies and British North America – owed their slave systems to the British. By the eighteenth century, the British carried more Africans than any other Europeans. Moreover British slave traders did more than simply provide their own colonies with Africans, for armies of slaves were shipped onwards from British colonies to other nation's colonies and settlements elsewhere in the Americas.[1]

The number of Africans sucked into this violent and destructive Atlantic system was enormous. Over the long history of the Atlantic system some 12 million were loaded onto the slave ships. At the height of Britain's slave empire, between 1660 and abolition of the slave trade in 1807, British (and British colonial) ships carried about 3. 5 million Africans across the Atlantic. By the height of that trade, some 40,000 Africans a year were transported to their enslaved fate in British ships.[2]

The Atlantic slave system had massive consequences for three continents. Firstly, Europe drew remarkable strength and material well-being from its slave colonies in the Americas. Europeans discovered, after experimenting with various labour systems (free and indentured labour, and mixes of both), that African slaves seemed well suited to their imperial ambitions of tapping the commercial potential of the Americas. Secondly, key areas of the Americas were utterly transformed by the importation and settlement of African slaves. Indeed it is often overlooked that more Africans than Europeans settled in the Americas in the years before 1820. Thirdly, swathes of Africa were seriously damaged by the haemorrhage of so many people, over so long a period.

African slaves and their descendants became a critical force in the shaping of the Atlantic economy. We need to remember however that the Atlantic slave trade was in full swing long before the British settled their own American colonies and that it continued (though under siege) for half a century *after* the British abolished their trade in 1807. Of course, the history of that trade was uneven, both across time and place. Nonetheless, this massive and quite unparalleled enforced movement of peoples was critical to the fortunes of three continents.

The precise details about Atlantic slavery have only emerged in the past generation, thanks to some remarkable research by a large numbers of historians. It remains unclear however whether these findings have yet made their full impact on historians of Britain. Historians of slavery and the slave trade tend to be specialists in colonial/maritime/American issues. Historians of Britain on the other hand have tended to view slavery as a distant, colonial or American phenomenon and therefore of only tangential interest to Britain itself. There are striking exceptions to this rule of course. It is also noticeable that a number of prominent Caribbean and American historians have long insisted that Atlantic slavery is a matter of great historical importance as much for Britain as it for the Americas.[3] But historians primarily interested in the *domestic* history of Britain have yet to incorporate slavery into the history of Britain in the seventeenth and eighteenth centuries.[4] Yet the recent findings of a number of economic historians have illustrated beyond all doubt that the transformation of Britain – the emergence of modern Britain – in the seventeenth and eighteenth centuries was inextricably linked to the Atlantic economy, at the heart of which was the slave trade and slavery in the Americas.[5]

The study of Atlantic slavery has, for perfectly understandable reasons, been prone to a process of fragmentation. It is so vast a subject (embracing three continents) over so huge a chronological period (in effect the best part of five centuries) that historians have, understandably, tended to fight shy of generalizations, opting instead for their own field of specialization. Most historians of slavery (like academic historians everywhere) work on rather narrow or specific studies. To impose shape and direction on so sprawling a subject, to make coherent sense of the whole, seems too daunting a task, and one moreover which runs against the academic historian's training of dealing with the specific and the particular. How can we integrate the *minutiae* of research on, say, African ethnicity with patterns of seaborne slave mortality, slave resistance on the plantations, or slaves' cultural habits on the very edges of American settlement? These examples – and many more besides – provide, at one level, fragments of an historical process perhaps best characterized by dispersal and fragmentation rather than coherence.

Fortunately, the pieces of this historical jigsaw have begun to take shape and to make greater sense in recent years – at the very time the data on slave history has become ever more specialized and abundant. A number of relatively recent intellectual and historical trends have begun to provide the tools which have enabled us to make sense of this sprawling subject.

Despite older traditional attempts at synthesis (influenced primarily by Marxist historiography) perhaps the most important recent step in this direction has been the growing acceptance of the concept of the African (or black) 'diaspora' to describe and explain the scattering of African peoples around the edges of European settlement. The study of the African diaspora is not, of course, simply the story of slavery – though the slave experience lies at the heart of that study. It might be useful at this point to illustrate the process by reference to my own work in the field, which began with two distinct studies, firstly in Jamaica, (and the history, written with Michael Craton, of Worthy Park Estate) and secondly, a study of the history of the black presence in England.[6] Both books involved key themes in the African diasporic experience – Africans displaced and transported against their will and shipped (in these two cases) to Jamaica and to England.

Thirty years ago, however, it was more difficult to see how these two separate stories fitted together. To put the matter crudely, what linked the history of Africans toiling to cultivate sugar in the middle of Jamaica with other Africans, at much the same time, labouring as domestics in fashionable English homes or working as sailors on board British ships? Was there an overall historical pattern? Today, thanks in part to the growing acceptance of the concept of the African diaspora, it is possible to see such apparent disparate elements as part of a more cohesive and integrated system.[7] Africans in their millions were removed from their varied homelands and shipped, enduring terrifying oceanic experiences, to all corners of European settlements in the Americas. Numbers of them, following the ebb and flow of European trade and migration, inevitably found their way to Europe. Though separated by thousands of miles, Africans in Lima and in London belonged to the same world of an African diaspora forged by slavery, and shaped and exploited by European and American interests for the economic betterment of Europe and white settlers in the Americas.

A number of the issues at the heart of the African diaspora have attracted my own historical interest in recent years.[8] In addition to studies which have tried to make general sense of the broader diasporic picture, I have also addressed a number of related specific issues within the history of Atlantic slavery. This book is the culmination of this research and seeks to confront a number of questions about Britain's slave empire in the Atlantic world of the seventeenth and eighteenth centuries. The single underlying theme is the attempt to suggest the integration of the British historical experience with events in the enslaved Atlantic; to suggest that Atlantic slavery was basic to British development, not simply on the high seas or in the Americas but, more directly, within Britain itself. Clearly, this is not to claim that the question of slavery was uppermost in the minds of British people in these years. Nor am I saying that the manifold consequences of slavery were the pre-eminent force in domestic British life in these years. But the book tries to illustrate the degree to which the slave empire, in all its forms, was a process which effectively intruded itself into British life, often in ways which contemporaries did not recognize. To use a phrase which haunts this book (perhaps too often for editorial satisfaction), slavery was out of sight and out of mind. But it was also inescapable. My purpose here is to suggest the importance of slavery in the history of Britain from the mid-seventeenth century onwards.

Part I
SLAVES

1 Slaves

In March 1797, a man in his early sixties died in Cambridgeshire, leaving an estate of almost £1,000 – perhaps £80,000 at today's values. He was, obviously, a reasonably prosperous man – and he was famous enough to attract obituaries in the London press. But what made him quite remarkable was that he was African. Born an Igbo around 1745 in what is now eastern Nigeria, he was seized at about the age of eleven and, like millions of others, dragged to the African coast, whence he was sold to a British slave trader. He was Olaudah Equiano, though throughout his life he used the name given to him by one of his subsequent owners – Gustavus Vassa. Shipped to Barbados, then to Virginia, Equiano worked at various enslaved jobs, on land and as a sailor, before arriving in England, buying his freedom, and establishing his fame, in the last decade of his life, as a literate, devout political activist, lobbying for the interests of the local black community and campaigning in print and in public for an end to the very system which had wrenched him from his home land – the Atlantic slave trade.[1]

At about the time Equiano was buying his freedom, one of his contemporaries, a London shopkeeper in Charles Street, Westminster, was making a modest living – like thousands of other London shopkeepers – by selling mainly tea, sugar and tobacco. While this affable shopkeeper chatted to his customers across the counter, his wife worked on a table behind him, chipping at the sugar loaves to make up the weights the customers demanded and packing his Trinidado tobacco into similarly appropriate packages. This man and wife team were examples of what Adam Smith and Napoleon called a 'Nation of Shopkeepers'. Like most others, this Westminster shop made a livelihood from selling tropical staples.

This particular London shopkeeper was different however. In July 1776 he began a correspondence with Laurence Sterne in Coxwold, introducing himself to Sterne with the startling words,

> I am one of those people whom the vulgar and illiberal call 'Negurs'.[2]

This shopkeeper/correspondent was another African, Ignatius Sancho. Born on board a slave ship in mid-Atlantic, Sancho was destined for Grenada; his mother died shortly after his birth – his father promptly killed himself. Sancho – recently the subject of an exhibition at the National Portrait Gallery – was, like Equiano, a former slave. Both men were literate and devout.

Were these two men, Equiano and Sancho, mere curiosities – unusual, untypical Africans, cast ashore in England along with the flotsam and jetsam of

Britain's massive Atlantic empire in the mid-eighteenth century – or do they represent something else, something more significant, more symptomatic of British experience? They were, after all, only two men (though we know of many other Africans living in England at much the same time). It is important to locate them more specifically.

Equiano and Sancho were two men among millions of Africans ensnared in the Atlantic slave system. Historians continue to debate the precise numbers, but the rough outlines are clear enough. From the Portuguese and Spanish origins in the sixteenth century through to the final days in the 1860s some twelve million Africans were shipped out of Africa and across the Atlantic. The first Atlantic slave trading was more in the form of piratical attacks on coastal settlements. But as the trade grew, it spread clean along the West African coast, from Senegambia to Angola and round to Mozambique. It reached ever deeper into the African interior, ensnaring whole societies and communities, either as traders or slaves. And all to deliver healthy young Africans to the European merchants and captains at their chosen spots on the coast. Like millions of others, Equiano had travelled for months from deep in the interior before he saw the Atlantic or encountered his first white man and the amazing sights of European sailing ships. What followed was, of course, that pestilential oceanic crossing of up to twelve weeks, in physical conditions that can scarcely be recalled. And all this was before the Africans staggered ashore to begin a lifetime's labour. If, that is, they survived. About one third died within three years of landfall (mainly from ailments contracted in transit).

Historians can calibrate the statistics of the crossing – the deaths, the illnesses, the packing, the profits. What we are unlikely ever to be able to do is to portray some sense of the mental trauma visited on all survivors. If we need confirmation of this fact we need only dip into slave popular culture and, more recently, the creative writing of African-American writers to catch some sense of the psychic scars which the crossing left to this day. We need also to remind ourselves that this was an experience which was endured by twelve million Africans.

The British did not initiate or pioneer the Atlantic slave trade – though they quickly came to appreciate its economic potential. But it was the British who honed and perfected the trade in humanity to unprecedented levels of efficiency and profitability. The Atlantic trade became an industry which lured ever more British ships, and traders. Between about 1690 and 1807 (abolition) some 11,000 British ships headed for the slave coast. These ships were a floating cornucopia; bursting with the material goods and benefits of an expansive British economy. All those goods were desired and consumed by Africans – in return for African slaves.

Even the ways the slave voyages were financed and organized give clues to the pervasive attraction of Atlantic slavery to British investors. Historians have tended to look to the obvious profit-makers in slavery – the stately homes built on the backs of slavery, the library in All Souls College Oxford funded by Codrington plantation in Barbados. Yet slavery was a system which seduced British people *of all sorts and conditions*. We know of a slave voyage funded by a range of local backers:

a widow with her inheritance, shopkeepers with a few pounds to speculate, merchants with more substantial funds, apprentices even, sinking their spare cash into the ship. On top of that, local carpenters donated their labours and time in return for potential profits.

We need then to think of Atlantic slavery as an economic attraction with an appeal which went far beyond the rich and famous and the commercially successful. This trade in African humanity lured the British in their droves. The end result was that, by the 1760s, British ships were ferrying 40,000 Africans each year across the Atlantic.

But what was it all for? Why pack millions of Africans into European ships and transport them to alien lands thousands of miles away? What lay behind this enforced oceanic migration?

We cannot begin to understand the history of Atlantic slavery unless we place it in the context of New World development and settlement. Put crudely, the African was the key pioneer across key regions of the Americas – especially the tropical and semitropical regions where land was plentiful and fruitful but where labour was scarce. Behind the impulse to import Africans there lay another, equally grim story. That was the fate of the Indian peoples of the Americas. From the first Spanish contact with the Indian civilizations – the Taino in the Caribbean, the Maya in Central America, the Aztec in Mexico, the Inca in Peru – through to the disasters which befell the Indian peoples of the Great Plains and the US South West a mere century ago, the story of the American Indian forms a litany of disease, death and collapse. This is not the place to try to tell their story. But it was the inability of the Indian peoples to cope with the disease of the invading Europeans and Africans which reduced their numbers to a pitiful level. European settlers quickly appreciated that local Indians would not provide labour for whatever economic development (mining at first, plantations later) they embarked on. But there, on the other side of the Atlantic, was Africa, already tapped for labour by the Portuguese and Spanish, in the Atlantic islands and in the Iberian peninsular. With the coming of sugar cane to the Americas and the development of the first labour-intensive sugar plantations, the fate of the Africans was sealed.

Over the next three centuries, the very great majority of all Africans shipped across the Atlantic were destined, in the first case at least, for work in sugar plantations. Sugar cultivation began in Brazil, later shifting to Barbados and then Jamaica and gradually seeping throughout the tropical regions. And all for what? To satisfy a voracious European appetite for sweetness in all things – an appetite which had not even existed before the opening of the Americas. Later, once it had proved its value as a way of breaking open the land and organizing labour, the plantation itself became the spearhead of European settlement; for tobacco in the Chesapeake Bay region of Virginia and Maryland, for rice in South Carolina, for cotton, in the nineteenth century, along the line of the advancing American frontier and later still for large-scale agriculture clean around the world, from South Africa to Fiji, from Malaya to Hawaii. But in these early years, the plantation proved its value – to Europeans at least – through sugar production.

Sugar cane, like black and white humanity, was imported into the Americas from elsewhere as part of 'the Columbian Exchange' – the transfer of humanity, flora and fauna from one part of the globe to another. The combination of sugar and African labour transformed not only critical swathes of the Americas – from Brazil to the West Indies – but it changed forever the tastes and social habits of the wider world. By the mid-eighteenth century, the West Indian slave colonies had sweetened British taste, in all classes and regions, in both food and drink. Indeed the British sweet tooth had become an unquestioned fact of life. Much of British social life was punctuated and dictated by routines which depended on sugar.

When we consider those common images of British social life by, say, 1750 the picture become clearer. Fashionable ladies entertaining friends to tea, the sugar bowl a vital component in the table arrangements. Crowded coffee shops, especially in London but throughout urban society. Coffee – thick, black and naturally bitter in taste – was laced with sugar cultivated by black slaves in the British Caribbean and in all the coffee shops the atmosphere was thick with smoke from tobacco grown by imported Africans slaves and their descendants in Virginia and Maryland. We might even stretch the point a little further, by standing outside most front doors in the city of York today and, if the wind's in the right direction, enjoying that sweet chocolate smell wafting from the city major chocolate factories. When Cortés made contact with the Aztec empire, the Aztecs consumed their chocolate mixed with chillies and peppers. The Spaniards changed all that by adding sugar grown by Africans in other parts of the Americas. It was that *mixture,* the blending and creation of cultural taste in the early white settlement in the Americas, which formed the basis, ultimately, for the great chocolate industries of the modern world (founded, curiously, in England by a troika of Quakers – Fry, Cadbury and of course Rowntree).

This sweetening of Western taste was made possible by African slaves. The people whose empire hinged on African slavery – the British – developed the greatest craving for sugar. By the mid-eighteenth century the British were infamous for their sweet tooth. Dip into contemporary books of household management (themselves so emblematic of domestic prosperity and consumption) and the sugary phrases leap off the pages: 'Sweeten to taste'. It was no accident that the British had a communal sweet tooth, for they, more than any other European people, had brought into being and perfected the largest of slave empires in the Americas. It was the British who carried more Africans into bondage than any other maritime nation and it was the British who consumed the fruits of slave labour in ever growing volume. The British by 1750 simply took for granted the exceptional – and utterly new – fact that sugar was a basic aspect of their collective social make-up.

By the mid-eighteenth century, the British had secured their position as the unrivalled power in the Atlantic. Much of that power was directed at securing the lines of defence of empire and commerce between Britain, Africa and the

Americas. Here was the lucrative axis of British eighteenth-century commercial and global power. And the lubricant of that axis was the wretched African slave.

To get some sense of this we need to look at some figures. By 1820, something like 12 million people had migrated across the Atlantic to the Americas. Of that total, about 2 million were Europeans. The rest – 10 million – were Africans. It was a vast, miserable movement westwards, millions of people scattered across the face of the eastern Americas, none of them knowing where they were, deracinated from everything familiar, arriving alone, with no kin or family, near-naked and invariably sick.

Atlantic slavery was a violent institution. It was conceived and nurtured in violence, it was maintained by the threat and the reality of violence and many slaves clearly came to think that violence, on their part, was perhaps the only way of challenging slavery. Yet it has been too easy to see this violent, predatory and abusive world as the *only* reality of black slavery. We now know that beneath its undoubtedly exploitative surface, slavery offered its victims scope for personal and communal action and development which few historians once thought possible. Black slavery soon slipped its moorings in the sugar fields, and spread rapidly throughout the colonial Americas. As colonial society matured, black slaves could be found in most walks of life. Skilled men and women in town and country: carpenters and masons, gunsmiths and seamstresses, musicians and drovers, hairdressers and publicans, sailors and traders.

Take again, the case of Equiano. Enslaved at eleven, by the age of twenty-one he had saved enough cash to buy his own freedom – at a cost of £70. To celebrate his freedom he spent another £8 on a new suit of clothes and threw a party for his African friends. Where had all that money come from?

In fact, like armies of other slaves, Equiano made the most of every commercial opportunity which came his way. As a young slave sailor, he earned a few pennies shaving other sailors. In his travels as an enslaved sailor he noticed that glassware was cheaper in St Eustasius than in Montserrat, so he bought cheap and sold dear between voyages. In a month he had made a dollar from an initial three penny investment. He carried oranges and limes from one island to another and sold barrels of pork in the same way. He took turkeys from South Carolina to Montserrat. When he signed off from a ship in London in 1767 Equiano had £37 in his pocket. In the last decade of his life, he accumulated substantial savings by publishing his own autobiography, and promoting it vigorously across Britain.

By then of course he was a free man; it could be argued that Equiano was unusual. But the closer we look at slave society, the more extraordinary the picture becomes. Throughout the Americas slaves engaged in varied economic activities on their own behalf, the profits and fruits of which enhanced their private, family and communal lives. From Brazil to Barbados, from Jamaica to Virginia, whites and visitors were astonished, throughout the history of black slavery, at the elaborate, colourful and costly celebrations organized by slaves, for birthdays, high days and holidays, for crop-over, Christmas and New Year – and for a host of African ceremonies that whites preferred not to think about too closely. Fancy suits and complex dresses, costly shoes and whimsical hats. And all this from people who spent their working days in rags, from people who, in the case of the Africans, stumbled ashore from the slave ships alone, sick and virtually naked. Again, where did it all come from?

It came of course from the slaves' own efforts and initiative. We need not think of slavery consuming all the slaves' working hours. Sometimes – and for some – it did. But in agricultural work growing sugar, tobacco, rice or cotton nature imposed its own quieter periods. Moreover, even the harshest of slave owners came to recognize the importance of free time or rest periods and rewards. At those moments slaves turned to their own gardens and plots, tended their animals, developed their own crafts and skills. And from their own activities there emerged the foodstuffs and meats, clothing and furnishing which were then traded, bartered and sold – for cash, for other items or for favours. Gradually slaves were able to fill their homes with more than life's bare necessities, with clothing, furnishings, tableware, even, in the case of the Bible, with books. We know for example that in 1800 about one fifth of all the spare cash in Jamaica was in slave hands. Equiano, again, had a chest for his money. We know of slaves who lent money to their masters, who sold animals to neighbouring white men. If we need to catch a glimpse of this independent slave culture at work, we need only look at the graphic images of slaves heading for market, weighed down with fruits and vegetables, with animals and artefacts of all kinds, all of which was for sale. And the slaves returned home, weary, but with the profits of their own labours. Then, the day after, they were back in the fields – back in their ragged clothes and once again under the watchful eye of their owners and drivers.

Slaves *owned* things; they improved their lives and shaped a personal and cultural environment which often seems out of kilter with slavery itself. In its diversity and complexity, the material culture of slavery often surprises the historian.

Slaves travelling to market provide just one example of slaves on the move. Yet slaves have too often been viewed as static, anchored to their plantation from arrival or birth to death. Some, obviously, were, but many moved around. Slave colonies throughout the Americas were swarming with slaves on the move. Drovers handling the beasts; dockers loading the ships bound for Liverpool, Bristol and Glasgow; slave sailors like Equiano, plying their maritime trade in the Atlantic routes, between islands and between North America and the Caribbean. Slave stewards were common on British warships. Cooks and servants travelled to markets and towns in the slave colonies to haggle and buy. Equiano, for example, visited more than thirty countries or settlements, between his native African homeland and the Arctic.

In fact, slaves were peripatetic – people on the move – to a degree historians have often overlooked. This physical movement of slaves was critically important to the slave societies. Travelling slaves brought news, gossip, tittle-tattle from distant places directly into the heart of remote slave quarters. Slaves in Jamaica soon heard about the London campaigns against the slave trade. Blacks in London similarly picked up news about slaves on the far side of the Atlantic. In the linguistic blender of the slave colonies – where every European language mixed with a galaxy of African tongues and every conceivable shade of local *patois* – words travelled faster than we might expect, from Africa, to the Americas, to Europe. It was impossible to staunch this flow of news and rumour, just as it was impossible to stop slaves moving.

Perhaps the most disturbing aspect of the slaves' movements (at least to their owners) was that slaves regularly took flight, normally for a few days, though sometimes for a long time and occasionally permanently. Colonial newspapers are filled with advertisements for runaway slaves. Historians used to view slave runaways as people escaping *from* something – from a harsh master or mistress, from the scene of their latest humiliation or pain. Now, we are as likely to think of them running *to* someone, especially to loved ones. Many runaways were simply heading for a lover or for family – husband, wife, parents – seeking the company of dear ones scattered by the inevitable enforced separations that were among the most hated of slave experiences throughout the Americas. Slave voices bitterly recalling the pain of separation from loved ones remain the most anguished of slave testimonies.

This should not really surprise us of course. But what is unusual about these terrible stories is that Africans had stepped ashore alone. Africans were not (as a rule) bought or enslaved in family groups. They were deracinated, from place, from people, from kinship and community. Yet, within a generation, these same people had formed rudimentary families, and the consequent families formed the social structure of slavery itself – the slave community – which proved critical to slave life throughout the Americas. The very worst punishment owners could dole out to their slaves – and they thought long and hard about how to refine their punishments – was to damage the slave family. And because slavery was an economic institution, because owners needed to get the most out of their human investments, family life was often damaged by sale and relocation. But through it all, the slave family survived.

This story of black slavery unfolded, in the main, in the Americas: in Brazil, throughout the West Indies and in what was to become the USA. Because it was so far away from the European heartlands, it has long been tempting to think of it as out of sight and out of mind. British historians have often talked and written of slavery as something *over there* – in Africa, on the Atlantic, in the Americas. Yet the more we know about slavery and the more we seek to trace the links between Europe/Britain and slavery, the clearer it becomes that Britain was intimately involved. Slavery was *British* as much as it was American. Most slaves – unlike Equiano and Sancho – did not come to Britain. But slave labours, the fruits of their efforts, the profits from their toil, certainly did find their way to Britain. We cannot, for example, abstract slavery from the history of Liverpool – with its thousands of slave voyages in the eighteenth century. We cannot remove slavery from the history of Glasgow – rising to prominence as it did on the tobacco trade from the Chesapeake. And how can we ignore slavery when we look at those sugar bowls, tobacco pouches and pipes displayed in museums up and down Britain. How can we *not* notice Britain's slave history when we look at the people who live in Britain's former slave colonies? And of course, since 1945, closer to home in Britain itself?

These last points touch on something more fundamental than the history of slaves or the history of Britain. What they raise are questions about the nature of Britain's recent past and the shaping of British collective national identity. What makes us what we are, how we see ourselves and how others see us, is so obviously the creation of history over a long span that it seems scarcely worth making the point. But too often the dominant tendency has been for the British to think of themselves relatively unaffected by the wider world, to see domestic history as just that – something local, home-grown, parochial even. True, there is the related trend to see the British *influencing* the outside world. But this is a view which makes little sense when standing in the middle of, say, Kingston Jamaica, or Bridgetown Barbados – or when visiting surviving plantations in South Carolina or Virginia.

Let us try to give these broad issues a particular, individual focus. Let us go back to a five year period between 1789 and 1794 when Olaudah Equiano's autobiography was one of the best selling books in Britain. His book established his fame in the 1790s, when the British were locked into their titanic struggle with revolutionary France. At times, the nation teetered on the edge of starvation. Searching for ways of feeding the poor, social observers were both irritated and confused by the universal working class attachment to drinking tea with sugar, both commodities imported huge distances. And who produced that sugar? The Africans and their descendants, 5,000 miles away in the West Indies.

These were the people who, as we have seen, not only transformed great swathes of the Americas but also helped to change key features of British life itself. What is more, we need to think of this slave experience as part of a broader African diaspora – the scattering of millions of Africans across the face of the Americas and Europe – and all for the material betterment of their white owners and masters (and mistresses). At the time Equiano had made his name in London, in the late 1780s, some of his fellow countrymen had even been settled in the first convict colonies of Australia. They were rebellious, resistant slaves, too tough or difficult to contain even in the Caribbean, shipped to the hulks in London and thence to the penal colony of Botany Bay. True, there was only a handful. But the fact that they were there gives as clear a sign as possible of the reach and spread of the African diaspora. What has not been mentioned through all this are the consequences for Africa itself. What did this haemorrhage of millions of people do to the various societies of Africa affected by the massive slave system sponsored by the European presence on the West African coast? It is a question which, whatever the state of historical investigation, is unlikely to go away in the near future..

2 Slavery, commerce and the slave ships

Black slavery lay at the heart of the late eighteenth-century British Atlantic empire. It dictated the pace and direction of much of the flow of people and goods along those complex trading routes which were, at once, the lifeblood of empire and the sustenance of expanding metropolitan business, trade and taste. It was also a system which, crucially, intersected with and depended on an even wider global commercial network that stretched from China to the interior of Africa. Within a mere fifty years, however, the slave system was utterly transformed. On the eve of American Independence, few could contemplate British life without the slave empires of anglophone America. By 1832, British slavery was doomed.[1]

The human statistics provide a simple framework. Whites outnumbered blacks by two to one in the British Americas by 1776, but such figures can deceive. Since the early seventeenth century some 815,000 whites had migrated to the British settlements – compared to 2,339,000 African slaves. Few have noticed the central fact that, by 1780, 'In sheer number of settlers, British America was actually more black than white.'[2] Of course the Africans and their local-born descendants (who inherited their mothers' bondage) were spread unevenly through the region. They were concentrated overwhelmingly in that string of possessions across the Caribbean sugar islands (territories greatly augmented by the gains of the Peace Treaty of 1763) and in those mainland settlements which had flourished on the back of plantation-based staple production, notably tobacco in the Chesapeake and rice in South Carolina.

Africans were imported into the Americas to work for their (mainly white) owners. Whatever else they achieved (normally under the most testing of social and physical conditions) they were valued – and prized – for their labouring strengths and skills. In time, slaves came to fill a remarkable range of occupations in the Americas – from gunsmiths to cowboys – but initially the Europeans wanted African muscle power. In the pioneering days of settlement, Africans worked alongside Europeans and local Indians, cutting back the wilderness and bringing the land into fruitful cultivation. From one colony to another, the first years were uncertain and survival unsure. Once the ideal local economic formula had been discovered however, once the most suitable export crop had been planted, slavery developed as the backbone of the local plantation system. Nowhere were the slaves more visible, more spectacularly successful (for others, if not themselves) than on the sugar plantations of the Caribbean.

The sugar islands struck visitors as an image of Africa, their large-scale plantations worked by large gangs of slaves (contemporaries often used military imagery to describe slaves at work). Slaves worked at appropriate tasks from childhood to old age. As the settlements matured, slaves acquired that range of skills necessary to all rural industries and to local society at large. The sugar industry of the late eighteenth century for instance required more than simple muscle power for its economic success, and much the same was true of other slave-based economies. In tobacco, rice and a host of other crops throughout the Americas (cotton, indigo, coffee and chocolate), slave skills and experience were crucial ingredients in local economic success.

The whole edifice of British Atlantic slavery hinged on two main factors: regular supplies of new Africans delivered by the slave ships, and markets for slave-grown produce. It was, however, a remarkably complex commercial empire (so often misrepresented by the concept of a 'triangular trade'), for each point of the trading system was linked to a much broader system of global trade. Stated crudely, the Atlantic slave empire was but one element of a massive global trading system which stretched from the furthest points of Asian commerce to the unknown point of enslavement deep in the interior of Africa and on to the insecure frontier of the Americas. Africans, for example, were bartered for and purchased at myriad spots on the sub-Saharan coast, in return for a multitude of commodities culled from Britain's relentless global trade. Indian textiles, French wines, English metalware, cowrie shells from the Maldives; all and more were handed over in return for cargoes of African slaves.

For all its inhuman cruelty and violation, the British trade on the African coast had, by our period, become a well established and sophisticated branch of maritime business. From Sierra Leone to Angola, slave traders roamed the coast, dealing with communities of resident Africans and Europeans (and mixtures of both) for coffles of slaves acquired from the interior. The African coast was environmentally dangerous for Europeans and took a horrific toll of white sailors and traders. Such risks however failed to deter the flotillas of European slave traders arriving in growing numbers throughout the period. Moreover, European losses and sufferings were as nought compared to what happened to the African slaves consigned to the terrors of the slave ships.

The African survivors of the horrors of the Atlantic crossing (ten millions plus) were destined to produce tropical staples for western consumption. Of all the slaves landed in the Americas, some seventy percent were destined to work in sugar, a crop which, more than any other, utterly transformed the taste and social habits of the western world. Sugar cane, like the black and white populations of the Americas, was an alien, transplanted commodity. By the early eighteenth century, however, slave-grown sugar had made that leap, so common to a host of tropical staples, from luxury to necessity.[3] What had once graced the tables of only the rich and influential was now to be found in the humblest of homes and could be bought for pennies from the meanest of local shops in the most inaccessible corners of the British Isles.[4] Sugar was an additive for ever more foodstuffs but it was its use as an ingredient in drinks – most notably of course tea – which secured sugar's pre-eminence. The West India lobby, that nexus of planters, shippers, financiers and agents which formed so powerful a group in mid-eighteenth-century London, was keen to promote tea-drinking. The more tea the British consumed (secured from traders in Canton) the more sugar was required from the slave fields of the West Indies. And the same was true of those other tropical drinks, notably coffee and chocolate, so recently adopted by Europeans. All were naturally bitter drinks, made palatable to western taste only by the addition of sugar.[5] And *that* was made possible by the transportation of Africans into the tropical colonies of the Americas. Tea from Canton, coffee initially from the Yemen, chocolate from Aztec Mexico, sugar courtesy of African slaves in the Caribbean – here was an illustration of the complexity of international commerce which underpinned slavery itself.

The British consumption of slave-grown produce increased remarkably in the eighteenth century. In 1700 the British imported 23,000 tons of sugar. A century later it stood at 245,000 tons.[6] Much of that sugar was stirred into tea, a habit which had taken root in the years 1685-1700, thereafter remaining a characteristic feature of the British social landscape. In the 1720s some 9 million pounds of tea came to Britain. That rose to more than 20 million by the 1740s and stood at 37 million pounds at mid-century.[7] Because of high excise duties, a thriving tea-smuggling industry conspired to bring the British consumer enough tea to be able to consume more than two pounds per head annually.[8]

Drinking sweetened tea became a habit which brought more than mere pleasure, for it transformed the routines of domestic life and shaped key areas of sociability. The pattern of the day came to be structured around a host of tea-drinking rituals, from the fashionable tea parties of ladies of sensibility[9] (displaying the finest of imported 'china') through to labourers interrupting their toils to drink sweet tea. The paraphernalia of tea making became a basic feature of British private and public life. At first, imported Chinese porcelain was – like sugar and tea themselves – costly and beyond the reach of all but the wealthy. As the volume of imports increased, such artefacts became cheaper. Chinese porcelain was, by the early eighteenth century, imported by the ton; a 40-ton lot in 1718 contained 332,000 pieces. When, in 1791 the East India Company stopped importing Chinese porcelain, an estimated 215 million pieces had landed. By then, such tableware had found its way into almost every corner of British domestic life.[10] It was a commercial route followed by British imitators, notably Josiah Wedgwood.[11] By the late eighteenth century, these once-exclusive artefacts of tea-drinking (teapots, sugar bowls, teacups) were to be found on even the humblest of British (and American) tables.[12] To satisfy the same cravings, these same staples and tableware were also shipped to the most distant of British postings and settlements on the very edges of empire and trade. Frontier settlements the world over, from Australia to Canada, enjoyed their sweet tea and tobacco much like the British at home.

Sugar, then, had brought about the most spectacular consequences in Britain. But other slave-grown staples also proved instrumental in redefining both taste and social style. Tobacco for example was as British as sweet tea by the mid-eighteenth century. Here was another domestic custom made possible by the slave empires of the Americas. Sold in ale houses, coffee shops and apothecaries, tobacco was also readily available from the proliferating number of specialist shops, markets and pedlars. When a man could not afford his own pipe, he could smoke from the communal pipe passed round in the place of drink. And all of this was made possible by the slaves of Virginia and Maryland. The 65,000lbs of Virginian tobacco exported to England in the 1620s had risen to 220 million pounds fifty years later, a massive expansion made possible by the switch from white indentured, to enslaved African labour. To populate the rapid expansion of the Chesapeake tobacco plantations (generally much smaller than the sugar plantations of the Caribbean), Africans were shipped in, sometimes from the West Indies but mostly direct from Africa. Between 1690-1770 some 100,000 slaves found themselves deposited in the tobacco-growing region.[13] Their labour generated a massive export of tobacco, costs fell and, despite hefty duties, British consumers had, by the early eighteenth century, become addicted to smoking on a lavish scale. Their habit was sustained (as was their taste for sugar) by a national network of thousands of small shops whose main source of income was the sale of the recently established exotic and tropical staples.[14]

As the smoking habit spread across the social divides, from the rich and the exclusive, tobacco lost its initial social cachet. By the mid-eighteenth century, the dense unpleasantness of tobacco smoke had led to its exclusion and segregation in fashionable homes. The emergence of a more refined sensibility in propertied circles served to curb female smoking. Female snuff-taking remained fashionable however: Marie Antoinette received gold snuff boxes on her wedding to Louis XVI, and George III's Queen was known as `snuffy Charlotte' because of her fondness for snuff. Again, fashionable usage soon spread through poorer circles and by the end of the eighteenth century, snuff-taking (though normally from humbler, less costly snuff boxes) had filtered down the social scale.[15] As with tea, the social consequences of tobacco went far beyond the smoker. Smoking became a manifestation and reflection of contemporary eighteenth-century masculinity. Women – certainly ladies – did not smoke. Those who persisted were unladylike, refusing to abide by a convention which had so recently come to shape the nature of feminine behaviour. Some women of course *did* continue to smoke, notably among the lower orders. But few were in any doubt that they, and their habit, were unladylike. By the late eighteenth century, artists and writers were apt to depict old age and poverty as an old woman with a pipe in her mouth.[16]

By the late eighteenth century tobacco consumption had become progressively more masculine, aided in large measure by the influence of the military (notably the Royal Navy) and the fact that, during that century of ubiquitous warfare, so many men spent time in the military. Here was a simple Native American crop, once culled from the wild and now disciplined and cultivated by slaves throughout the Chesapeake, which formed the foundation of a massive transatlantic business, with repercussions which stretched from the most miserable of American slave huts to the emergent prosperity and physical grandeur of late eighteenth-century Glasgow.[17] Tobacco was even used to pacify

Africans on the Atlantic slave ships. Throughout colonial America, slaves – male and female – took comfort in the pleasures of a pipe. But the consequences of tobacco-smoking were to be seen most dramatically in Britain (and Europe in general).

By the end of the century, tobacco's role as a masculine pleasure was secure. By then, of course tobacco also had created all the results familiar today. It blackened teeth and congested the smokers' lungs. Doctors reported that chronic tobacco addicts were afflicted by permanent coughs and spitting.[18] But who, in the smoke-filled conviviality of the local ale house or coffee shop stopped to think that all was made possible by the labours of slaves in the Chesapeake? Once again, here was a product of the slave empire and global commerce which had so deeply embedded itself in British daily experience that its social and economic origins passed unnoticed

The fruits of slave labour had been intruded into every conceivable cranny of British domestic life by the end of the eighteenth century, following that familiar trajectory from initial luxury, affordable only by the rich (and promoted by apothecaries as a solution to a host of pains and ailments) to become the unquestioned, cheap and universally available necessity in the homes and public venues of even the very poor. In times of hunger and hardship – especially in the crisis years of the 1790s – commentators (notably Sir Frederick Eden) were both perplexed and irritated by the poor's attachment to the consumption of staples imported from the far reaches of the world. It is easy to see why hostile critics felt that the British people – of all sorts and conditions – had become addicted to luxuries, to fads and fancies shipped at great costs from the far reaches of the world . Their forebears had managed quite well without them. But those same forebears had not been a powerful, imperial and maritime-trading people and it was in that role that the British people of the eighteenth century had become attached to tropical produce and hence to the slave empires of the Americas. To add to the curious complexity of the issue, the two most important of such consumables – sugar and tobacco – were cultivated by slaves who had *themselves* been imported vast distances and at very considerable cost. Even today, the human and economic formula of the British slave empire in colonial America looks bizarre. Yet we need to remind ourselves that what lay behind these apparently innocent aspects of domestic consumption was the exercise of British imperial power and commercial dominion which enabled the British to transplant peoples and commodities from one side of the world to the other in a complex commercial exchange shored up by maritime power – and all for the economic betterment and daily pleasure of the domestic population.

The economic vitality of the American slave colonies was maintained by ever more Africans shipped, in unspeakable conditions, from the African slave coast. With a few exceptions (Barbados most notably), slave populations of the islands failed to increase naturally. Problems of sexual and age ratios, infertility, high mortality and a host of ailments (all in a context of harsh work in an alien environment) served to prevent normal, healthy slave reproduction. Cruelty played a part of course, though by mid-century all but the most callous of planters were coming to recognize that they needed to care for their slaves, if only to get the best economic return on their investments in human capital.[19] From first to last, West Indian planters and their British backers cried out for still more Africans.

The ending of the original monopoly system of supply and the opening of the slave trade to competition (though within the restrictions of contemporary mercantilist ideals) created a gathering rush of slavers, investors, ports and associated British industries to satisfy the slave owners' needs. In the first half of the eighteenth century, British slavers delivered some 20,000 Africans each year. For the rest of the century the figures rose to between 35-40,000 annually. Between the end of the Royal African Company's slave trading monopoly in 1698 and the abolition of the British trade in 1807 perhaps 11,000 ships were dispatched from England to trade in African slaves. They transported about three million slaves in that century.[20] London led the way, followed in the early eighteenth century by Bristol (with its ready-made advantages of maritime links to the west). But by about 1750, the growing city of Liverpool had become the nation's pre-eminent slave port. Almost half of all eighteenth-century English slave ships sailed from Liverpool. In the last generation of the slave trade, something like three-quarters of all the English slave trade was fitted out in Liverpool. By then, that city had become the undisputed slave port of Europe.

Liverpool – like Bristol – had extensive maritime trade elsewhere of course – to Ireland and southern Europe, to North America and to the fisheries of Newfoundland and Greenland. Slave trading was only one aspect of the expansive maritime trade of the eighteenth century. Yet it was the African slave who became 'the corner stone of Liverpool overseas trade from about 1730 to 1807. ' Something in the region of a third to a half of all Liverpool's tonnage in the eighteenth century was concerned with the slave trade and its related maritime ventures.[21] The African trade was irresistibly seductive – replete with commercial potential – notwithstanding the ubiquitous dangers of disease, warfare and slave revolt.

The slave trade spun a commercial web which ensnared many commercial interests far removed from the centres of maritime life. Deep in the hinterland of the nearest slave port, manufacturers and producers, shopkeepers and farmers found themselves supplying the slave ships. The trading system on the African coast and the Caribbean islands devoured British goods on a remarkable scale. The islands were especially demanding, requiring items of every conceivable kind to feed their slaves and to maintain the plantations to a level of profitable production.[22] Here was a commerce which attracted a complexity of local backers, suppliers and investors, all keen to put their money, produce or skills into the fitting-out and loading of a potentially profitable trip to Africa and the Americas. It is tempting to discuss the major British ports, (and it is true that they dominated the slave trade) but there was a multitude of smaller ports dispatching a regular flow of ships in search of African slaves; from Preston and Poole, from Lyme

Regis and Bideford.[23] Whatever the risks, however frequent and disruptive the impact of warfare (much of that warfare of course aimed partly at maintaining or enhancing British imperial and slave trading dominance), the prospects of slave trading profits were enough to spur British slave traders and their multifaceted backers to dispatch ships into the Atlantic.

As the eighteenth century progressed, slave ships became bigger and more costly. In the mid-eighteenth century the average cost of a slave ship and its cargo was about £4,000 (two thirds of the cost being in cargo). By 1800 that had risen to upwards of £12,000. The total sums invested were enormous. Something like £1,000,000 a year was invested in the slave trade in Liverpool alone by 1800. Much came from smaller speculators though substantial investments were from the wealthy in the north-west. At the heart of Liverpool's financial support for slaving lay an elite of Liverpool business families.[24]

The Atlantic slave trade did more than profit its lucky, or persistent investors. It served to recast the face of eighteenth-century Britain, often in ways which remain unrecognized. Its most obvious impact took the form of those bands of ex-slaves cast adrift in British ports – the human genesis of the first British black communities – cast ashore in Britain as a result of British maritime trade and power. The slave trade also enhanced the material prosperity of British ports. Profits for the slave trade hovered at around 10% by the late eighteenth century and those who stuck with their investments saw their family/business fortunes mount. From the Atlantic trade they were able to acquire those trapping of eighteenth-century material well-being disgorged with ever greater abundance by consumer industries on both sides of the Atlantic. The most successful constructed city-centre homes brimming with the most fashionable of fittings, they built business headquarters of the most elaborate kind and enjoyed regular trips to the most fashionable of watering-places. Indeed, the vulgarity and opulence of slave-based wealth became something of a caricature among observers of social life at English spas (notably Bath).

There was , then, a widely diffused interest and investment in slave trading which manifested itself in a multitude of forms across the face of eighteenth-century Britain. The results of the commerce in humanity could be seen on all hands. Nor was it restricted to those people most obviously profiting from the trade. From the craftsmen who built and equipped the ships through to distant suppliers of goods for the ships holds, all and more found their interests intimately linked to the prosperity spawned by slavery. This coalition of interests formed an entrenched (and socially varied) lobby across Britain, ready to offer a fierce defence of slave trading when the early abolitionists raised their initial objections in the 1780s.

Key areas of British economic and social life had been refashioned around certain items wrested from fruitful tropical or semitropical soils by the lifetime efforts of imported slaves. The pattern recurred time and again. Whenever a new tropical commodity was found to be commercially viable, attempts were made (not always successfully) to shift production to slave colonies. Cacao for chocolate

– found by the Spaniards among the conquered Aztecs – was now grown in the Caribbean slave islands. Coffee, once restricted to the Yemen and consumed in a string of Levantine communities, was transplanted to slave production (it was ideally suited to the higher altitudes of the mountainous islands where it grows to this day). Tobacco, previously a ragged weed, plucked from the wilds by Indian peoples throughout the Americas, was transformed by carefully managed slave cultivation in that fruitful Chesapeake region of Virginia and Maryland. Rice, now shifted from Africa to South Carolina, was used extensively for starching fashionable clothes. In all these cases – and there were more – the sweat of distant slave labours benefited domestic British life.

But who so much as thought of these slave-based origins? Understandably, slavery went unchallenged, by and large, because it was out of sight and out of mind. When the initial moral and religious objections were voiced against the slave trade and slavery, those early abolitionist voices were easy to ignore or dismiss because slavery yielded such material bounty and pleasure to the British. To criticize the slave empire was to threaten the pleasures and the profits of metropolitan Britain itself. Yet at the very height of slave-based imperial prosperity, critics began, from 1787 onwards, to make their anti-slavery views heard.

In 1787 a small band, mainly of Quakers – men of sensibility, who approached slavery from varied religious and humane positions – formed a committee in London to demand an end to the Atlantic slave trade. It must have seemed a forlorn hope. Within a mere four years however they were able to muster more than 500 petitions from across the face of Britain, with 400,000 names objecting to the slave trade. It was an extraordinary – and quite unexpected – salvo against a slave lobby which had assumed that its business was secure because it contributed so massively to Britain's well-being. No one could predict the matter, but within a generation the slave trade, the umbilical cord of British colonial slavery, had been cut. Slavery itself survived until the 1830s. (The progress of abolition can be followed in Chapter Six of this book.)

The abolition of the slave trade in 1806-1807 cut the supply of African slaves, and ultimately transformed slavery in the colonies. Planters had to treat their slaves differently in order to make the most of their human capital. There were other changes however which few could have predicted at the time. The decline of the older African, and the rise of local-born, population in the islands compounded many local tensions, especially those expectations among local-born and skilled slaves for preferential treatment and better prospects. The planters' need for field hands however served to frustrate those ambitions. Caribbean tensions were compounded by the development of a political debate in the islands which embraced black and white and which was partly literate and enhanced by the rapid flowering of West Indian newspapers throughout the islands. Most important of all perhaps was the dramatic rise of local (mainly nonconformist) churches among the slaves and the swirl of abolitionist news from Britain.

The revival of the British abolition campaign after 1824 fanned the embers of slave discontent (which had already erupted in Barbados in 1816 in a revolt – for that island – of unusual savagery). It witnessed a miserable reprise of a familiar tale: black grievances, an initial slave outburst, suppressed by plantocratic and colonial violence on a massive and (in British eyes) horrifying scale. The pattern was repeated, with even more horrible consequences, in Demerara in 1823 and, most savage of all, in Jamaica in 1831-32. Slave resistance of course had been as characteristic of colonial slavery as plantocratic violence. But the revolts of the early nineteenth century were different. Viewed from Britain, they seemed a throwback to a world which had long gone, to massive social discontent, savage suppression and legalized violence of a kind not seen since the Scottish and Irish troubles of the previous century. To a society progressively influenced by a new sensibility about matters of cruelty, the fate of the West Indian slaves seemed unjustifiable. And all for what? To maintain an economic system which was itself increasingly prone to economic criticism.

The churches formed the key element. Tens of thousands of slaves were now Christian, caught in that web of nonconformist organizations and belief which had been spun by missionaries throughout the islands and which had links to their mother churches in Britain. Slave congregations, slave preachers, biblical imagery to advance the cause of freedom – all and more served to integrate the progress and fate of West Indian slaves more closely into the considerations of domestic British congregations. When the British read about the slaves (or listened to preachers returning from the slave islands) in the 1820s and 1830s they viewed them as persecuted co-religionists. There was then a rising sense of outrage among British congregations about the fate of West Indian slaves. Treatment which had once gone unchallenged – the everyday stuff of slavery – now seemed utterly at odds with a changed Britain. Here was a slave system which could only be kept in place by the most fearsome application of state and plantocratic violence. More and more British observers felt that it was not worth it.

The campaign launched against colonial slavery from the mid-1820s turned to well-tried abolitionist tactics. It was carried forward by that much deeper surge of reforming sensibility and organization which was most striking in the campaign to reform Parliament. The tactics, personnel, even the vocabulary were similar. Grass-root pressure persuaded MPs to adopt slave emancipation and the declining band of parliamentary defenders of the slave system found themselves harried inside and outside Parliament. It was, however, the reform of Parliament in 1832 which sealed the fate of British slavery by changing the electorate, curbing the power of Old Corruption and enfranchising newer sectors of the population. The numbers of emancipationist MPs increased and their pro-slavery opponents were reduced – in numbers, power and persuasiveness. With Parliament reformed, it was but a matter of time – and detail – before British slavery was given the parliamentary *coup de grace*.[25]

Why should the capitalist metropolitan power, so enriched throughout much of the eighteenth century, turn, so quickly and so vigorously, against the institution which had yielded such profit? That slavery remained profitable up to its dying days (its most active participants were after all loudest in its defence) merely compounds the dilemma.[26] Slavery was, to repeat, only one of a host of congruent issues which focused on freedom. Freedom of labour, of capital and management to conduct their economic lives untrammelled by restrictions and controls, was the very essence of a new kind of British economic power. After 1776, thanks to Adam Smith, it was also the core of a new economic thinking. To attack slavery was to advance a new social and economic orthodoxy by asserting the primacy of freedom in all things.

In all this, the temptation is to see things narrowly, to view black freedom (conceded partially in 1834 and completely four years later) as a metropolitan concern. Yet the slaves were clearly an agent in their own freedom, for it was the changes in Caribbean slave societies that persuaded more and more people in Britain that slavery was doomed. The slaves were, increasingly, Christian. The most impressive of slave forums was that proliferation of congregations across the islands in which slaves expressed themselves in a biblical vernacular (if not a style) familiar to any British observer. News from slave communities quickly filtered back to all corners of Britain. Equally, news from Britain seeped into the slave quarters, bringing encouragement and the conviction that salvation was in sight, that the local, white oppressors were out of kilter with the changing mood in Britain itself. When slavery passed into oblivion (in the British Empire at least – elsewhere it survived for another half-century), 750,000 freed slaves celebrated in and around their churches.

Here was an institution – slavery – conceived and maintained in conditions of extreme violence but which ended peacefully. Black freedom also heralded the precipitous economic decline of the former slave islands. Those planters still in need of malleable labour persuaded the Colonial Office to recruit indentured labour from India (creating a system which survived until World War I). Such changes failed however to prevent the rapid decline of the economic power and influence which the Caribbean had once mustered in British imperial affairs. Soon it was hard even to imagine how important the islands had once been. As the British looked elsewhere for trade and dominion, the Caribbean seemed little more than a troublesome backwater – a reminder of a former, but now redundant empire. What had made the West Indies so important – so crucial an element in the eighteenth-century imperial scheme of things – was their centrality in a much broader global economic system. Slavery belonged to that broadly based Atlantic empire which formed the heart of the old imperial system. The 'triangular trade' is a crude way of expressing a complex network on which had been created a major trading system linking Britain, Africa and the Americas. It was a system moreover which was related to the trading networks of the wider world. Though British interests, after 1838, looked elsewhere for profitable trade and dominion, it is clear beyond doubt that the old Atlantic empire, its foundations secured by enslaved humanity, was the rock upon which much else was constructed. The legacy of slavery lived on of course, most notably in the form of the communities of free black peasants of the West Indies. But it survived much closer to home – in the habits of the British people themselves. The fruits of slave labour had shaped key habits and addictions of the British people (and, increasingly, of millions round the world). What could be more British than a sweet cup of tea?

Tea drinking rituals are so established a feature of British life that tea, and all its associations, have become something of a caricature. Yet these rituals are British only by adoption – by historical accident. They came into being at a specific historical epoch and were shaped by a series of contingent historical factors. And, as with so many other features of everyday British life, they were intimately involved with British maritime experience. In those extraordinary episodes of populist nationalism which are periodically orchestrated in Britain (the `last night of the proms' being an obvious example), the words of the informal national anthem, *Rule Britannia*, are sung with gusto and approval. The line proclaiming, `Britannia rules the waves', looks rather threadbare today but when first performed, in the 1740s, it expressed strategic fact. And the waves which Britain ruled, and which the Royal Navy took such vigorous action to secure and defend, formed lines of global trade and commerce which linked the imperial heartland to the profitable and much-prized colonies and trading stations around the world. The cornucopia of tea from China, sugar and rum from the Caribbean, pelts and furs from the Indian peoples of North America, British produce shipped by the boatload to West Africa and the Americas, all and more were secured by British maritime power. But nothing was so prized and jealously protected as the trade in African slaves. It was the sweat of those Africans and their descendants, toiling in the sugar and tobacco fields of the Americas, which made possible the luxuries which the British (and other Europeans of course) enjoyed at home.

In the course of the history of the Atlantic slave trade (which lasted effectively until the 1860s) more than ten million Africans survived the horrors of the Atlantic crossing. Millions of Africans did not survive that maritime journey, while others died within Africa, *en route* to the coast. They were the victims of kidnappings and of internal warfare, much of it prompted by the demand for slaves on the coast itself. The Africans were terrified when they first caught sight of the ocean and of the ships riding at anchor. The early piratical capture of slaves gave way to complex, but very different, systems of buying slaves. Some were sold from custom-built forts (a number of which still survive). Other were sold in local towns and cities. Still others were sold from beaches (much depended on the local geophysical conditions). But all slaves were subjected to similar humiliating and intimate inspection as traders tried to calculate their value and to barter that value with the goods from the ships arrived from Britain or elsewhere. Slave ships spent weeks on end sailing up and down the coast, buying a few slaves here, a handful there. But the longer they stayed on the African coast, the higher the death rate among the crew – and among those slaves already packed below.[27]

The Africans (a majority were always male) were manacled and shackled together and lodged below decks, as their numbers increased, in those conditions of inhuman horror well known because captured by the cross-section graphic representations of the late eighteenth century. When the ships were ready to head westward into the trade winds to cross the Atlantic, the slaves' sufferings , already serious on the coast, began in earnest. Chained together, pitching and rolling across the ocean, the living, the sick and the dead side by side; chains chafing and sore, all of them wallowing in the stable-like filth of the slave decks. Fed communally from bowls (distributed to ten to twelve slaves, feeding themselves by hand) it was only a matter of time before ailments set in. The commonest complaint was dysentery – `the bloody flux'. If the weather was bad, the depleted crew were hard pressed to sail the ship, leaving little time to care for the slaves in their squalid sufferings below decks.

Many Africans fell ill, many were depressed, some went mad. Slave ships were rigged around with nets to catch those slaves who sought to end their suffering by plunging into the sea. And the crew could never allow slaves on deck in any numbers without their shackles, for fear of violence and insurrection. Time and again slaves tried to rear up in defiance; time and again they were violently put down. Indeed the slave ships became infamous for the violence and sexual attacks inflicted by the crew on the slaves – though some captains sought to prevent them (if only for economic reasons). But we need to recall that in the initial dealings between black and white – at the point of inspection and sale on the coast and in the Atlantic crossing, the formative exchanges were characterized by violence. It was an apprenticeship for the life of a slave in the slave colonies.

The duration of the crossing was critical. The worse the weather, the longer the crossing, the worse the sufferings of the slaves. For a start they were neglected by the hard pressed crew. The longer the crossing, the more likely it was that food and water would begin to run short (the captain having loaded provisions in the anticipation of a particular duration for the Atlantic crossing). In recent years historians have produced specific information about the details of the Atlantic crossing: the timing, the packing, the death and illness, the levels of abuse. But what no one has calibrated (perhaps because it will always remain incalculable) is the mental anguish which *all* Africans suffered as they pitched their miserable way to the Americas.

The slave ships were, at once, instruments of excruciating torment for millions of Africans and the cause and occasion of profit and pleasure to the European backers. The agonies of the slaves were forgotten, overlooked (out of sight and therefore out of mind) by those Europeans who came to depend on, and to enjoy the produce created by, the sweat of imported Africans. Who so much as thought about the Africans in their hellish oceanic experience, when enjoying sweetened coffee in London's fashionable coffee houses in the mid-eighteenth century? Who gave a second thought to the African corpses cast overboard in mid-Atlantic, as Englishmen passed round the communal pipe of Virginian tobacco in the smoky conviviality of their nearest tavern? And who, when they looked at the expansive and prospering face of late eighteenth-century Liverpool or Glasgow, saw that behind their handsome new buildings was the misery of African slaves?

Not surprisingly, nightmares of the Atlantic crossing haunted the folk memory of slaves throughout the Americas. In their early days in the Americas, African slaves stayed close to their 'shipmates', those Africans who had endured and survived the Atlantic crossing with them. The ships, the ocean, the traumas of the slave-deck remained lodged in the communal memory. It was a trauma which, though many recovered from it after a fashion, became part of the slave persona. Time and again, slaves returned to what had happened to them on the Atlantic. Their tales of the sea crossing, passed on to their children and the local slave community, became a defining fact of slave life. It also became a critical element, for good or ill, in relations between black and white, in slavery and in freedom.

Landfall in the Americas did not bring an immediate end to the slaves' sufferings. The indignities of intimate inspection began all over again, as the crew prepared their African cargoes for sale to the critical purchasers waiting at the quayside. The planters, agents and others, though often desperate for new slaves (especially in the West Indies and Brazil – less so in colonial North America), were alert to the problems and human defects created by the Atlantic crossing. Though the ships' crews cleaned up the slaves, glossed their skin with palm oil, gave them tobacco for pleasure, and generally tried to shake off their communal misery, potential buyers were not so easily deceived. Once again, African slaves were treated like cattle in an auction. Sometimes the sales were held on board the ship, sometimes in a neighbouring pen or yard. Sometimes, the slaves were already assigned to particular purchasers. But the confusions, the separations, the noises and the physical assaults – of slave owners physically grabbing the Africans they wanted – served once more to terrify the weakened and depressed African arrivals.

Most of the new slaves were sick, mainly, as far as we can tell, from their sufferings in transit. They now found themselves separated from friends and the shipmates they had made on the voyage. It was as if life's miseries would never end. More than that, for some, the journey had not ended. Some of course were taken to plantations close to the point of sale. But many were transhipped to distant parts of the same colony or onto smaller islands. Others were reloaded into a different vessel for the onward voyage to North America and the tobacco fields of the Chesapeake region. We need to recall however that of all the Africans shipped across the Atlantic, seventy percent were destined, in the first instance at least, for work in the sugar colonies (an indication of course of the remarkable importance attached to sugar itself in the broader Atlantic economy).

We know of individual slaves sold on to more distant colonies, whose relief at landfall in, say, Barbados, was quickly cast out by the distress of a renewed oceanic voyage. Even then, when landed along the myriad waterways which feed into the massive expanse of Chesapeake Bay, the Africans were marched on, to their new home in tobacco country. Once there, they had to buckle down as quickly as possible to a lifetime's labour (and learn the *patois* of local slaves and white people). All too often, the slave's safe arrival was short-lived. A very high proportion died within the first three years of landing in the Americas – mainly from the ailments which they had contracted at sea and had imported into the Americas. Many were too deeply anguished to slough off their gloom and despair. Whatever the cause, armies of African slaves died within three years of arrival. And so the planters had, once again, to look across the Atlantic to the slave traders to fill the gaps – to import yet more Africans to step into the ranks vacated by the dead Africans. It was a system with a deathly circularity. The more Africans imported, the more died from their illnesses, the more their purchasers had to turn, once again, to Africa for replacements.

Yet, from the agonies of these arrivals there emerged a series of slave communities throughout the Americas, communities which, though designed for the economic interests of the European settlers, came to provide a richly textured society for survivors and their offspring. In the slave quarters – which differed from place to place – slaves created for themselves a local culture which was distinctive but which clearly drew inspiration from varied African pasts. It also returned, time and again, to the experience of the Atlantic crossing. In folk tales, in popular memory and, more recently, in the imaginary reconstruction of the slave past, the slave ships have figured prominently. How could it be otherwise?

We need to recall the enormity of this experience. There were, to repeat, some ten million African survivors of the Atlantic slave ships (and a similar story could be told for Africans shipped from Indian Ocean ports). For them, the memories of Africa were mediated by the seaborne horrors on the Atlantic. More than that, the initial, formative contacts with white people were shaped by the experiences of enslavement on the coast, by consignment to the pestilential hell of the slave decks and the weeks of oceanic misery. All long-distance oceanic migrations were of course fraught with dangers and traumas for most people in the days of sail. What we need to recall is the formative role which this agonizing oceanic crossing played in shaping the lives and the subsequent culture of African-American life in the Americas.

3 Sugar and tea

In that brief period between the end of the Anglo-American war (1783) and the outbreak of the French Revolution (1789) the British seemed unchallenged in power and presence in the Atlantic world. With the loss of the American colonies, the focus of British power – naval, strategic and economic – was the Caribbean, though in fact the West Indies had long formed the core to British strength. The precise centre of that power had shifted from its initial location in Barbados to the larger, more dynamic island of Jamaica. But whichever island we care to pinpoint, the region as a whole formed the source and occasion of British global power. Guarded by the (now) undisputed strength of the Royal Navy, serviced by armadas of commercial vessels criss-crossing the Atlantic, the British West Indies disgorged commodities (and prosperity) to the booming ports and hinterlands of the metropolis, on a scale, and with ramifications which even today beggar belief.

Here was a massive, international system which shaped, defined and confirmed British Atlantic pre-eminence. It was a system – a process – which locked together varied societies on three continents (Europe, Africa and the Americas) into an intimate mutual dependence. But, as we shall see, the ramifications of the Atlantic system went even further. Goods, profits and commercial links with Asia were also tied into the Atlantic system. Indian textiles, transhipped through Britain, clothed African slaves in the West Indies. Cowrie shells from the Maldives were used in barter for the exchange of slaves in the West Indies. What had emerged, on the back of African slaves in the Americas, was an economic nexus with extraordinary global reach and consequences. And it all hinged on sugar.[1]

In the course of the Atlantic slave trade – from its immediate, tentative, post-Columbian origins, through to its dying days in late-nineteenth-century Cuba and Brazil – the main engine which drove boatloads of Africans across the Atlantic was cane sugar. Of the more than 12 million Africans loaded into the pestilential hell of the slave ships, some 70% were destined to work in cane fields. Of course millions were directed towards other slave labours – from sailors to seamstresses, from artisans to interpreters, from nurses to cooks.[2] There were few jobs in the colonial Americas which failed to attract slave labour, and we must avoid the temptation of thinking of slavery solely in terms of heavy field work. Nonetheless, if any single crop devoured the imported Africans, it was cane sugar. Of course sugar itself also spawned a myriad occupations and skills in and around the sugar plantation.

Here then is a remarkable – and central – historical fact: the cultivation of a commodity (which was itself alien to the Americas) by enslaved labour which had itself been shipped thousands of miles, on American lands seized by invading

Europeans, and all to satisfy a taste for sweetness in Northern Europe (thence clean round the world).

It is tempting to take the universal taste for sweetness for granted, to assume that the voracious, late eighteenth-century appetites for sweetened drinks and foods were natural and normal. But whatever their deep-seated physiological impulses, and however traditional or universal sweet tastes in varied societies, the mass consumption of cane sugar represented a new, qualitative shift in western habits.[3] There had, quite simply, been nothing like it before; no taste concocted so swiftly, dramatically and ubiquitously, from a distinctive set of social circumstances. Nor had there been anything quite like the Atlantic slave system which effectively gave birth to this taste. We need, then, to make the link; to look behind the obvious social *manifestations* of eighteenth-century sweet tastes (sweet tea/coffee, the ubiquitous sugar bowl, sugar on sale in contemporary shops) in order to tease out the defining global context. Put simply, cheap accessible cane sugar was a function of British economic and colonial power. But who thought this, who thought about the slaves – the instruments of sugar cultivation – when adding sugar to their tea or coffee in eighteenth-century Britain?

The geopolitical formula which made this possible is clear enough. It had a pattern which remained much the same from one region to another, throughout the rise and fall of different European powers, as colonial domination and Atlantic pre-eminence passed from the Spanish and Portuguese, to the Dutch and on to the British. American land, effectively purged of its native peoples by complex processes of imported diseases, armed might and in some cases incorporation, was transformed by European settlers. Backed by varied metropolitan financial and mercantile interests, sanctioned by European states (and state power) and secured by emergent naval and maritime strength, the Europeans transformed critical areas of the tropical and semitropical Americas (in Brazil and the Caribbean).[4] The Europeans tried a host of crops, cultivation methods and labour systems. But it was the transplanting of sugar cane to Brazil (later to Barbados) and the use of the plantation for sugar cultivation that paved the way for the sugar revolution.[5] The plantations had of course already served a similar purpose in sugar cultivation in the Mediterranean and on the Atlantic islands.[6] But the sugar plantations of the Americas were characterized, from an early date, by the drive towards enslaved African labour. The exact point of departure – the moment when planters opted for slave rather than free or indentured labour – varied greatly. But sugar, with its labour-intensive demands, provided the critical impulse. Brazil showed the way, and by the time the emergent British had settled their own islands in the Caribbean in the 1620s (trying a range of other crops at first) the African slave was a feature of sugar production in the Americas.

The European involvement with African slavery was a tortuous affair. Few now doubt the existence of forms of African slavery long before the hesitant maritime arrival of Europeans in West Africa. Europeans tapped into those labour systems just as they locked into local economies and commodities (gold, wood, dyes) for their own advantage.[7] Initially used in the Atlantic islands and the Iberian peninsular, African slaves were transferred to the embryonic settlements of the Americas. Although marginal at first (on shipboard or in the Americas) African slaves proved their value on Brazilian sugar plantations from the mid-sixteenth century onwards. As the volumes of sugar exported to Europe increased and were transhipped from Lisbon to northern Europe, the European appetite for sweetness expanded.

The British came late to sugar cultivation. Equally (and despite early piratical ventures in the sixteenth century) they came late to African slavery. But the transformation of Barbados, from an island of small-holdings to an island dominated (by the 1640s) by sugar plantations (which, in turn, grew ever larger through a process of consolidation), pushed the British to the forefront of sugar production.[8] They consequently became major importers of African slaves, initially courtesy of Dutch slave traders (just as Dutch finance, experience and encouragement had helped secure sugar plantations in Barbados itself).[9] The subsequent rise of British power, the seizure of Jamaica in 1655 and the rapid development of the Jamaican sugar plantations brought the process to fruition. By the last decades of the seventeenth century, an increasingly powerful British state was able to orchestrate and finance the shipping of ever more Africans to the slave plantations of Jamaica. Their labours disgorged a vast and growing volume of sugar for the refineries in British ports, notably London, Bristol and (from the mid-eighteenth century onwards) Liverpool. Though the British centre of the slave trade shifted, the critical financing of shipping, of insurance, of cargoes and of commodity imports and processing remained in metropolitan hands. Yet the dominance of a small group of major merchants and backers can also deceive, for the British involvement in slavery quickly seeped into all corners of British commercial and economic life[10] In the process the British became the pre-eminent Atlantic slavers of the eighteenth century. Their ships (increasing in numbers) carried more Africans, more quickly, more effectively and more profitably than any other fleets. It was fitting – perhaps inevitable – that the British should in the process develop the sweetest tooth of all Europeans.

The accountancy of this process is, as we might expect, remarkably complex. Rather than seek a simple balance sheet – a profit/loss account of the system – we might be better advised to explore the *pervasiveness* of the economics of slave-based sugar. And whichever location we care to explore in the geography of Atlantic slavery, we are confronted by evidence of material well-being and economic advantage accruing to Britain from its involvement with the Atlantic slave system.

Take the case of the West Indian plantations themselves. Jamaica was the jewel in the West Indian crown by the mid-eighteenth century, its slave-based wealth disgorged by myriad plantations. One which exemplified the island's history under the British was Worthy Park, established in 1670 and located at the geographic heart of the island. It was in many respects a perfect illustration of the story of sugar, produced by its army of slaves (upwards of 500), managed by a small handful of whites, its produce consigned to Britain in return for regular imports of vital goods. Each year the plantation ledgers revealed a remarkably extensive litany of imported goods: tools for the slaves, clothes, hats and fabrics for slave dress, firearms for the whites, metal goods for the factory and farm, seeds for the fields, foodstuffs for black and white alike.[11] Scarcely a single facet of daily social and labouring life, for black or white, was unaffected by imports from Britain. Indeed life on that plantation – as most others in the region – could not have functioned without goods imported from Britain and from North America (and some transhipped from other countries). And all for what? For the annual production of sugar and rum, cultivated on Worthy Park's fertile lands by the slave gangs and consigned to British merchants. There, at what was the very epicentre of Jamaican slavery, both slave and free depended on Britain, on goods imported from Britain (and from further afield). Life on the sugar plantation was unimaginable without the regular arrival of British ships, loaded with the manifold artefacts of the British economy and keen to return quickly to British ports with slave-grown produce.

If we switch our historical attention to the imperial heartland itself, we can see the same process at work, of ports and their broader economic hinterlands vitally linked to the servicing of the African and West Indian trades. It is a story most graphically illustrated at the British docksides, where the massive proliferation of ships (and shipbuilding), dockside facilities, maritime manpower and the movement of goods to and fro attested to the buoyant vitality of the Atlantic trades. Whichever ports ships sailed from, heading for West Africa and the Caribbean, their holds were filled with produce and goods from the immediate dockside and from the regional hinterland.

The obvious story of sugar in Britain tells only part of the remarkable impact made by that commodity on British life. Sugar had, by the mid-eighteenth century, intruded itself into the most private and domestic recesses of British life. It had found its way into the kitchens and larders of British people of all sorts and conditions, had secured a special place on the shelves of tens of thousands of British shops and had secured a critical role in a host of private and social ceremonies. Indeed, sugar had become so deeply ingrained into a number of British social customs which survive to this day that it is easy to overlook their specific historical genesis. The rise of sugar was intimately linked to the rise of British tea consumption. The West India lobby actively promoted tea production, for they realized that expanding tea-drinking meant increased sugar consumption. The graphs and indices of British tea and sugar imports and consumption chased each other from the late seventeenth century onwards. Yet here was a curiosity, for the tea, imported vast distances from China by the East India Company (and purchased in exchange for valuables imported into China) was not consumed in its home region with the addition of sugar. Like all major exotic beverages which took hold in Europe from the sixteenth century onwards (coffee from Arabia, chocolate from Mexico) tea was drunk in China as a bitter, unsweetened drink. But in the course of the seventeenth century, Europeans, led by the British, transformed tea consumption by adding sugar. In the very years the British began to turn to Chinese tea, they became the major producers of cane sugar in the West Indies. Thereafter, tea and sugar were inextricably linked in British dietary habits. This association, in general, went unremarked; it seemed a natural combination, like love and marriage.

The figures speak for themselves. The imports of tea and sugar rose dramatically in the late seventeenth century but behind those figures lay important shifts in domestic social and material life in Britain. Tea-drinking is perhaps best recalled through those displays of contemporary tableware – Chinese porcelain, Sèvres, Meissen and Wedgwood – now displayed in galleries and museums around the world but originally the fashionable centrepiece of (primarily) female sociability among the well-to-do. There, alongside the teapot, cups and saucers, are the sugar bowl and sugar tongs, indispensable in the making, dispensing and consuming of tea. Around such artefacts there emerged distinctive rituals of sociability – captured in any number of contemporary portraits – in the homes of propertied people, in urban centres or at fashionable watering holes across Britain.[12] The tea sets themselves guide us to some remarkable economic transformations. Not only did the East India company import 215 millions items of 'china' for the European tea drinker, but European pottery manufacturers quickly fell into line, aping the styles and commercial success of the potteries in distant Nanking. It was a process which culminated, in Britain, in the rise of Wedgwood and his staggering commercial and entrepreneurial success in Britain, Europe and even in the Americas. Staffordshire ware had even found it way into the slave cabins of the West Indies by the end of the eighteenth century.

As with tea and sugar, the unit cost of tea sets (along with other tableware) fell in the late eighteenth century. As artefacts became cheaper, they passed into the hands of lower income groups. By the mid-eighteenth century tea and sugar consumption was basic to the daily diet not merely of the well-to-do, but even of the poor. Indeed it was a source of bemusement – and some irritation – to social commentators that the poor expected and relied upon goods and commodities imported vast distances and at great cost. Here was a perfect illustration of much broader social changes in the seventeenth and eighteenth centuries; the transformation of key imported commodities from the luxurious to the necessary.[13] Time and again – especially in times of hunger and distress – commentators bemoaned the poor's attachment to tropical staples. For their part, the poor became so accustomed to such staples that, in times of shortage, they would use other items to simulate them; burnt bread could pass for tea, and even ground ivy, among Australian convicts, offered a passable substitute.[14] But whatever its form, tea ideally had to be mixed with sugar. There may of course have been a deeper physiological force at work here, the need for a quick fix of energy by the ingestion of a sugary beverage. But how did the habit emerge?

All the major exotic beverages arrived in Britain at much the same time – the early and mid-seventeenth century – and all began life as luxurious pleasures of the rich and eminent. They also arrived, from their varied homelands, via complex maritime and overland trading routes, often diverted and transhipped in another European city. In Britain (more precisely England) they gained popular currency in the years when the early slave plantations began to disgorge their first sugar harvests to British markets. The addition of cane sugar provided an antidote to the naturally bitter tastes of these drinks. Precisely why and how those habits spread down the social scale remains unclear, though we can speculate on possible conduits. The most obvious channel was the world of sailors and others engaged in overseas trade, men familiar with the quaysides of the Americas, Europe and the Mediterranean, where imported goods and strange habits (and exotic peoples) mingled one with another. There was also the world of European medicine and pharmacy (itself rooted in Arabic traditions), which readily incorporated and transformed hosts of new exotic commodities from all corners of the world, often blending them together in new amalgams that seemed more appropriate for this ailment or that problem.[15] There was also the (more troublesome) process of social emulation. Habits, possessions, customs, fashions, fads – all and more moved down the social scale, from royalty and aristocracy, through the ranks of the prosperous and the aspiring well-to-do, before finding a more broadly based constituency among low income groups. It is easier however to see how such habits were diffused among the wealthy and the propertied than it is to see how they spread among the poor.[16] One possible conduit was the servant class; that large working group whose social origins lay at the base of society but which found its daily work, and even its living quarters, among their social betters. Social habits and even material goods (clothes, tableware) were passed onto servants – thence to a broader plebeian social world.

Whatever the precise point and mode of contact, exotic goods were widely diffused among working people by the early eighteenth century. In the case of sugar, two factors drove the commodity wider and deeper into British society. Firstly, the unit cost fell dramatically. Sugar and tea (and the tableware needed to consume them) became cheaper. And the process was greatly helped by the rapid proliferation of shops in all corners of the kingdom, urban and rural, enabling even poor people living in the remotest of places (rural Wales, the Highlands of Scotland) to acquire tropical produce. Such produce could be bought in the smallest of volumes and packages (ideally suited to low-income groups). And we know that shopkeepers – especially in poorer shops – found that the backbone of their livelihood was in selling exotic produce. Cheap food and drink (often adulterated) in accessible form, broken down to the smallest of units, was available across the counter in local shops.

To add to the process, sugar made a major impact in two other venues. It was quickly added to the list of ingredients used in British cuisine, most notably (and persistently) in the British passion for sweet desserts and puddings. Thus, both tea drinking and cooking (but more especially baking) secured a role for sugar in British domesticity. From the sugar in fashionable and costly sugar bowls through to the packages of sugar kept alongside other ingredients in the nation's larders and kitchens, sugar had secured a `natural' place in British domestic life. It also played an important role in a more public sociability.

Sugar was at its most sociable in the nation's coffee houses, hundreds of which dotted the centre of English cities – especially in London. Indeed by the mid-eighteenth century the coffee shop had become inescapable. Coffee was dispensed to the male clientele, who added their chosen amount of sugar. Commerce, banking, insurance, news from the colonies and from the provinces, political gossip and idle chit-chat, all flowed through and around the nation's coffee shops. The coffee shops became the focal point for a distinctive pattern of public sociability (much as had been the case earlier in Islamic societies) which was primarily masculine, often commercial but overwhelmingly recreational. Within those coffee shops, men took their pleasures from commodities brought from the very edge of global trade and domination: coffee from Java and Jamaica, sugar from the West Indies, and tobacco from the Chesapeake. Male sociability in this, like the tavern and alehouse, the most public and open of venues, was conducted through the ingestion of tropical staples. Thus both at home and in public, the British people had, by the mid-eighteenth century incorporated (and transformed) habits of consumption derived from colonial life and trade, rendering them distinctively local. This world of British domestic experience – tea at home, coffee in the coffee shop – may seem utterly removed from the world of Atlantic slaves. Yet without the Africans (and their descendants born in the Americas), the seventeenth- and eighteenth-century sugar industry could never have emerged as it did. Moreover the European acquisition of Africans – the bartering for, and purchase of, Africans by Europeans on the African coast – was made possible by European (in this case British) economic muscle. The produce of the British economy, and commodities transhipped through Britain from Europe and Asia, formed the means of purchase and exchange in Africa itself, passing from British ships into the hands of African middlemen and thence into the varied African societies ensnared in the slaving process. There were of course major repercussions of this European trading presence in West Africa – most dramatically perhaps through the vast movement of firearms into Africa. But the broader process was a further dimension of the rise of material consumption – in this case in West Africa – for the material goods disgorged by the economies of Europe and their colonial settlements or trading entrepôts. Africans, and slaves in the West Indies, became attached to imported alien goods and the social habits they generated.

It was a curiosity that tobacco (slave-grown in the Americas) was shipped to West Africa, along with European pipes, to satisfy African tastes. Moreover this slave produce was distributed to Africans consigned to the floating prisons of the slave ships in the hope of moderating their shipboard miseries. Tobacco was also used to fumigate the slave quarters on the ships. Here was a simple example of the completing of the slave circle. Newly purchased Africans pacified and comforted, *en route* to American slavery, by produce which had come via Europe, but which had initially been cultivated by slaves in the Americas.[17]

The concept of a triangular trade is of course too geometrically neat to describe accurately the diverse movements and processes of the Atlantic economy. Ships and trade flowed back and forth, directly to and from West Africa, from Europe to and from the Caribbean, direct between the West Indies and North America. It was a complexity of trade routes which cut back and forth across the neat symmetry of the triangle formed by the broad bulk of the slave trade. But each flow of people and goods was locked into the overall economic machine of Atlantic slavery. And at each point of the Atlantic system we can see ample evidence of the powerful influence of a slave presence. Of course the most obvious result was the scattering of African peoples, not merely into the main concentrations of African slaves in the Americas, but also (in smaller concentrations) in urban settlements in the Americas , and even, by one remove, in Europe itself. The black community in London by the late eighteenth century is just one example of such migrations.

The man who came to be the spokesman for London's eighteenth-century black community, Olaudah Equiano, had once been a slave both at sea and on the island of Montserrat. There he had worked for his owner in the process of unloading imported supplies and loading sugar bound for Europe. He had also been employed as an interpreter and agent dealing with newly arrived Africans on the slave ships. Equiano, like millions more, had been caught up in a massive global system which, though spilling out in all directions, had been brought into being to create and satisfy the western craving for sugar. By the late eighteenth century sugar was so widespread, so universal among all sorts and conditions of people, that it seemed natural and unquestioned. It was, as we have seen, a function of particular historical circumstances and as it emerged, the story of sugar left a profound mark on the shaping of western life. Thereafter it flowed to all corners of the world, sweetening the tastes of people on all the world's continents. But the impact of this – the rise of the sugar complex – on Africa had yet to be fully explained. But sugar was only one of a string of tropical staples which embedded themselves deep in British social life in the seventeenth and eighteenth centuries. As the British became addicted to the habits of imperial conquest and domination, so too did they acquire the taste for the produce of distant empires and settlements. These `fruits of empire' established themselves as part of British domesticity itself. And all was made possible by Britain's slaves toiling on the edges of the expansive empire.

4 Slaves, free time and leisure

Few would dispute the violence endemic to the slave system. It was, indeed, a system conceived and nurtured by institutional and personal violence. Equally, it was unrelenting in the demands placed on the slaves. Yet, in time, the various slave societies accorded their slaves areas of freedom which historians have often overlooked. But does it make sense to speak of the leisure of the enslaved peoples of the Americas? How appropriate is it to use the concept of leisure in relation to millions of peoples whose purpose in life was simply to work for the economic betterment of their owners and masters/mistresses?

In fact, the most recent studies of slavery have spelled out, in fine detail, a general argument: that slavery in the Americas was too complex, too variegated and subtle an institution to be understood simply (or solely) in terms of the slaves' labouring efforts. To be sure, the Africans imported to the Americas, and their offspring born there were destined for work. But even the world of slave labours was itself more varied and nuanced than we once imagined. Equally, it is clear – and obvious – that even the most hard-pressed of slaves could not work *all the time*. Free time – evenings, weekends, holidays and high days – was an important aspect of slave life, more so as slave societies matured and took on more formalized routines and rituals, adopting or creating the calendars of local economy, agriculture or Christianity, quite apart from the residual African cultures transplanted and transformed into the slave quarters throughout the Americas. The critical question remains, however, can this free time, in which slaves created a culture of their own, be usefully or meaningfully described as 'leisure'? Before we can answer the question, we need to confront the broader historical debate about the history of leisure itself.

The history and sociology of leisure and related issues have attracted a remarkable upsurge in scholarly literature in recent years. Much of that literature has focussed on – often even defined – leisure as a function of industrialization. The material bounty which flowed, however unequally, from industrialization created leisure for millions, as distinct from the free time of pre-industrial peoples. Notwithstanding variations of interpretations, historians have come to accept that the modern, communal pleasures of people in the western world were qualitatively distinct from those of their pre-modern forbears; that the combined consequences of industrialization and urbanization ultimately (though slowly in many cases) enabled an expanding army of people to enjoy free time and spare cash as never before.

This distinction, between pre- and post-industrialization, is now recognized as too sharp. One result of research over the past twenty years has been to show that patterns of pre-industrial pleasures continued well into the era of advanced industry. Stated crudely, it is clear that 'modernization' did not completely succeed in purging society of its pre-modern indisciplines. In the case of Britain, critics of popular culture railed against the worst survivals of old customs well into the nineteenth century. The violence, blood-letting, animal baiting, and general undisciplined attachments of the old world survived into a period which prided itself on its civility and on the fact that it had turned its back on mankind's old, unpleasant pleasures.

The pioneers in the field of leisure studies were sociologists, followed, rather slowly, by social historians. The historical interest in leisure was, in the main, a by-product of the emergence of the new social history in the 1960s. Thereafter a growing number of historians turned to the history of leisure. Others of a more methodological bent sought a conceptual framework for the study of leisure[1] but even for those generally untroubled by theoretical issues, the question of leisure was not as straightforward as it seemed. If leisure meant simply time free from work – bestowed in abundance by modern societies – then it could be easily described and explained. But free time *tout court* is scarcely an adequate way of examining leisure; would leisure for instance encompass sleep or unemployment?

Few would doubt, however, that the combined forces of industrial and urban change had a transforming impact on the nature and course of leisure. Stated crudely, the people of the industrial world came to enjoy free time differently than their forebears in pre-industrial societies. Yet the historians of western leisure were far too often dazzled by the impact of industrial change. It seemed, at first glance, that the factory, the machine drove all before them. As ever more people found themselves rooted in industrial circumstances (even indirectly, or by association), the dictates of the machine (its disciplines, its imperatives, its mentality) and the association with ever-expanding urban life, utterly transformed the leisure pursuits of everyone. Just as working lives were transformed by industrial change, so too were leisure patterns. The turbulent games of the pre-industrial world (blood sports, folk culture, Shrove Tuesday football), were expelled from the face of urban society which demanded – and got – mass pleasures of a more orderly, controlled and acceptable kind.

Now, a generation on from those early histories of European leisure, the changes seem more gradual, less comprehensive than was initially imagined. For a start, until late in the nineteenth century, only a minority of people in the West found themselves caught up in modern industrial processes. Secondly it is clear that the presumed association between industrial and urban life was often more tenuous, less causal, than often alleged.[2] The mining industry is a case in point. Mines were normally located in a rural environment (mining villages). There, people in new, expanding industrial settings were in the midst of communities which were basically rural. Men whose work was, by definition, industrial developed patterns of leisure which were remarkably 'traditional'. Furthermore it is now clear that old recreational habits died hard in many of the new industrial settings. Rural habits, customs, traditions – of worship, of kinship, of association or pleasure-seeking – survived (though not always intact) and often became a distinguishing feature of life in new urban settings. Historians of popular culture now recognize the remarkable survivals of leisure forms throughout – and beyond – the period of urban industrial change. Industrial growth, far from driving a wedge between the modern and the pre-modern, often acted as a conduit for the continuation of social norms which survived, in transmuted form, from one social systems to another. Even that most popular of all global games, soccer, (now watched in its professional form by hundreds of millions of people) began life as a late medieval folk custom. It was transformed in the early years of the nineteenth century into its modern codified shape and spread throughout Western Europe after 1870. It may have seemed a different game, but it was recognisably similar to the games played across late medieval Europe. Historians of modern leisure have thus become as interested in the *continuities* as in the breaks between leisure forms across time.

The implications of the historiography of leisure for the study of slavery are profound, and warrant closer scrutiny. It is, however, a two way process, for what happened in the slave quarters of the Americas ought also to be of interest to students of leisure. How Africans and their descendants forged leisure pursuits for themselves from the most miserable and unpromising of circumstances raises interesting issues for students of leisure. Indeed the story of the slaves' free time poses a distinct intellectual challenge to those historians interested in the broader story of leisure itself.

It is easy to see why slave historians have paid less attention than others to the study of leisure. First and foremost they have, quite properly, been preoccupied with a very different historical agenda; with, say, the history of slave work, the demography of slavery and a host of its consequences. There has of course been an abundance of research on specific forms of slaves' non-work activities: on religion, material culture, on musical life and, increasingly, on economy and certain aspects of women's lives. This is however quite different from addressing the overarching theme of slave leisure itself. It remains true of course that we need to know more about the *minutiae* of slaves' free time – how they secured that free time, how they spent it, how they shaped certain areas of work to their own pace and intruded certain leisure forms (singing at work being perhaps the most obvious example).[3]

We also need to know more about the survival – though that term is problematic – of African aesthetics and customs transplanted and transformed in the Americas.[4] The durability of popular cultures in Europe in the transition from pre- to industrial communities offers a powerful suggestion that cultural habits survive the most fundamental and disruptive of shocks. Clearly, the traumas of the Atlantic crossing can not be equated with the impact of industrialization. But it might be time to consider the Middle Passage as much as a process of *continuity* as simply the means the severing of indigenous habits by the process of enslavement and oceanic transportation. Visitors to the Americas were struck, from one society to another, by the raw 'Africanness' of the slaves' communal pleasures. The sheer bulk and density of social evidence (from facial markings to musical expression) among the slaves force our attention to the continuities in slave social behaviour. Indeed, critics of slave life (most vociferously and often cruelly, the planters) imputed the worst of slave vices – the coarsest of slave pleasures, the most undisciplined and crude of enjoyments – to Africa. Though they wanted the muscle power of Africa, they disliked and feared most of the other human and social attributes which, they assumed, found their roots in Africa.

Perhaps no less interesting – and really only touched on so far – is that complex crossover of cultural influences between black and white which became so marked a feature of slave colonies throughout the Americas. In the search for African `survivals', or for traces of specific European influences in the developing, and distinctive cultural lives of slaves, historians have too often failed to notice the remarkable degree to which slaves influenced the whites around them. It was a recurring comment of visitors to English-speaking slave colonies that local whites seemed, in many key respects, like their slaves; they spoke like them, they enjoyed similar musical pleasures and often joined in many of the key public festivities which punctuated the calendar of the slave colonies. It was, to use the phrase of an historian of Virginia, a recreational world they made together.[5] Nowhere was this more striking than in the use of language. White children brought up by slave servants, '…have not an Opportunity of a better Education, in their Pronunciation, to speak in a drawling broken English like the Negroes.'[6]

One factor was pre-eminent in the development of slave recreational patterns, and remained so throughout the history of slavery. Work was the rationale, the very reason for the African presence in the Americas. However diverse and plural slave society became, work remained, from first to last, the foundation on which the slave systems were rooted. We know that slave work took a myriad forms, from the oppressive regimes of the large sugar gangs to the less malignant routines of non-gang, task and domestic work. Slave work was varied and diverse, shaped by the peculiarities of crop, geography and the time of the year. And since free time was afforded – or wrested – by the nature of work itself, the patterns of slaves' free time differed enormously. For rural slaves, the crop yielded its own free time, and at its own pace. The working day, the working week, the agricultural cycle and calendar created a framework around which working lives and free time evolved. Yet there were complications to this pattern. Throughout the slave colonies, the calendar of the Christian week intruded its own rhythm – long before many of the slaves formally adopted the religion which underpinned that calendar. After all, the whites and the plantation management shaped their own lives around that calendar (the week, month and year) and all derived from a European, Christian background. The Sabbath needed to accommodate itself (then as now) to the imperatives of rural and agricultural life; animals still need tending however firm the dictates to keep the Sabbath holy. African slaves were, from the first, obliged to adapt to a world with its own temporal patterns – dictated by Christianity and by the routines of local work.

Slaves' free time, then, was shaped by the particular combinations of local work and environment and by the calendar. It is also clear enough that, for all the gross and often violent exceptions, slave owners recognized (as did employers in pre-modern Europe) that free time was important not merely for the slaves but also for slave owners. Slaves who were granted free time and who were able to enjoy themselves as they saw fit, without the dictates of their owners, were better equipped for the inevitable return to work. The custom of granting free days to slaves varied enormously throughout the West Indian islands. But the general rule applied that free days and specific holidays were ubiquitous. Indeed, they became an important tactic in the manual of slave management. At this level, there was little difference from the world of pre-modern Europe, where customary rights conceded free days to labouring people in return for a renewed application to work (and social tranquillity) afterwards. Workers returned to work refreshed (or more likely, hung-over) and masters felt able to demand renewed labouring effort in return for their granting of free time.[7]

Free time for slaves was reciprocal: an acceptance by both black and white, for a brief moment, that the world could turn upside down. But it was granted on the strict understanding that the world righted itself at first light on the following morning. Masters who reneged on these customary rights – who expected slaves to forgo their free time for work – could expect trouble. Even those planters who granted their slaves time for their pleasures were relieved when the festivals passed trouble-free. One Jamaican planter reported that he was 'extremely happy to find that the Negroes have behaved so much to their credit during the Christmas Festival…'.[8] This plantocratic sigh of relief was echoed across Europe at the end of plebeian festivals when the world slipped back to normal.

One central problem in assessing slaves' free time is the fact that much of that free time was granted to allow them to work, in their gardens and provision grounds. The produce of that independent slave labour was, in effect, money saved for the slave owners. This scarcely seems like leisure. Where land for export staples was scarce, costly, or where planters had made the economic decision to let slaves cultivate their own food rather than provide it, a great deal of slave time freed from the planters' scrutiny was, nonetheless, destined for work. The freedom to work (in order to eat) sits uneasily with most accepted definitions of leisure. Yet even here, this world of independent cultivation (i.e. work) often fed into another area of slave independence, namely the ability to create foodstuffs or other commodities for barter, trade, exchange and sale.[9] From this independent slave economic activity there emerged that diverse freedom and enhanced economic power bestowed by the acquisition of material goods. Independent work bred material consumption. And material consumption created a degree of independence. The acquisition of money and goods – the entree to the world of material consumption – made life more tolerable (in some cases even comfortable), it enhanced a sense of independence and, most crucially, it enabled innumerable slaves to fashion for themselves cultural activities which, in time became part of the warp and weft of the sociology of slavery.

A few examples will suffice. Slaves charged with theft from other slaves in St Ann's, Jamaica, in the 1780s made off with a great variety '…of sundry Goods, wearing apparel and other Matters to a large Amount.' In addition to the usual clothing, food and eating utensils, one slave stole a clock – from another slave.[10] Even more eye-catching perhaps was the sight of 'a shelf or two of plates and dishes of queen's or Staffordshire ware' in a slave home.[11] It seems extraordinary that some of the artefacts of the material revolution transforming contemporary Britain found their way so quickly into the slave quarters of the Caribbean, among people we might expect to have little to show for their labours. Clothing and furnishings, instruments and animals, finery and necessities; all and more began to shape for the slaves a material culture which was more varied than we might initially expect.

Bryan Edwards was clear in his own mind that a process of 'civilizing' the slaves was underway by the late eighteenth century. And what underpinned that process was the urge to material acquisition. Unlike Sir William Young (who thought money itself was the civilizing force), Edwards argued,

> It is not therefore the possession of money alone; it is the new desires springing up in his mind, from the prospects and examples before him that have awakened his powers and called the energies of his mind into action.[12]

Historians of material consumption have only just begun to ponder the implications of the fact that West Indian slaves and North American Indian peoples were as hungry for new material artefacts as the plebeian town dwellers of Western Europe.[13] In the case of the slaves, the attachment to material culture stemmed from their own efforts – in their free time.

Slaves were granted free days from one island to another. But those free days were clearly spoken for; allocated to the various tasks (of self-support) which owners had devolved onto the slaves themselves. There were however other days – notably as a result of amelioration – which sought to guarantee free time/leisure in its full sense. Partly under pressure from the metropolis, convention was sharpened. Customary free days every two weeks became law. Saturday too came to be granted as a statutory day free from work. William Young noted in 1791 (of Saturday), 'This day (as usual) a half holiday from twelve o'clock, for the negroes.'[14] Workers in a wide range of British industry were still demanding the same concession – Saturday free from work – seventy five years later.

In the years after the Jamaican slave code of 1788, local slaves accumulated twenty-six free days each year, in addition to Sundays and other holidays. Again, it is revealing to recall that as late as 1834, clerks in the Bank of England received only four guaranteed days free from work.[15] In practice, as we might expect, slaves' free time varied greatly from one property to another. Slaves remained in the hands of men who saw fit to impose the laws to their own advantage, though even then, the granting of free time was recognized as a mutually beneficial process. Not surprisingly, too, such variations between properties was often the stuff of friction; what were slaves to expect by way of their customary and legal rights when they knew of peers elsewhere who enjoyed better (or worse) conditions? In reality, folk memory and practice was a powerful force. Slaves knew their rights and only the most foolish or desperate slave owner could hope to deny them without cost.

By the late eighteenth century, slaves in the British Caribbean appreciated that they had certain rights and access to free time. Though this might, in retrospect, seem a marginal benefit, on the very edges of a hostile and oppressive system, the slaves themselves sought to maintain, to preserve and when possible to advance those rights. Disputes over the right to have a Saturday afternoon free, or to be free from work at feast days on the Christian calendar (most notably Christmas and New Year) were not uncommon. It has been argued that slaves who lived closest to centres of urban life – where information and news were most readily available – were the ones most likely to be alert to their legal and customary rights.[16] And it is certainly true that new laws sought to tighten the controls over the free-time and movements of slaves who lived in or close to urban areas.[17] In truth, the slave awareness of such rights was contagious. The social history of slavery which has unfolded in recent years is of an institution which was porous to the movement of ideas and where the remarkable physical movement of slaves across the face of the islands, across the region (and even criss-crossing the oceans), in conjunction with the careless talk of their owners, ensured the rapid and ubiquitous flow of ideas and information. Word travelled fast and effectively from one slave quarter to another. Rights bestowed in one place were envied, sought or adopted in another. This, after all, was the pattern of customary leisure rights in Western Europe, where a series of local (generally parochial) customs and rights coalesced into a broader mosaic of conventional free time practices throughout a much wider geographic hinterland.[18] Masters who failed to conform to local customs were likely to find slaves taking matters into their own hands. Slaves simply failed to turn up for work on those days they deemed to be their own. When their concept of free time was transgressed, when individual owners failed to conform to local practice, popular usage might simply be enforced. Slave owners' determination to enforce work on those days clearly earmarked as rest days might prompt even more vigorous slave resistance.[19]

Here then is an illustration of that classic borderland dispute which served to highlight the nature of slavery throughout its history; the need to accommodate owners' rights and self-interest alongside slave conventions (which themselves hardened into rights over time). What might, at first glance, seem to be of mutual benefit (planters obviously benefited from a refreshed slave force returning to work from their rest) was often disputed terrain, where popular usage trespassed on the economic imperatives of ownership. The matter could not be easily resolved by simple application of force or by slave owners insisting on their rights over their servile labour. Slaves could, in that curious fashion which became a hallmark of slave societies throughout the Americas, safeguard their own collective interests by blunt refusal. In the case of free time, the fact that slaves often refused to concede their conventionally acquired free days to the *force majeure* of planters was itself an important insight into the slave mentality about customary rights, and especially into the importance they attached to free time.

The most striking attachment to free time was of course in those particular periods which formed the high days of the Christian calendar. It is surely significant that the slave attachment to Christmas in particular was in evidence *before* the slaves' conversion to their masters' religions. It was after all the Christian calendar which provided the temporal framework for the slaves. Sunday became the customary weekly day of rest, much as it did in Britain, with the further concession of half the day on Saturday. But the highlight of the slaves' leisure cycle was Christmas; the most important point of the Christian calendar became the highlight of the slaves' annual round of festivities. More than that, in the exuberance, colour and energy invested in that holiday season, the slaves (of the British Caribbean) again shared many of the elements of pre-modern people in Europe. Described in 1808 as a 'Saturnalia', the slave Christmas,

> seems to throw a veil of oblivion over their cares and their conditions; in short they seem as a people recreated and renewed.[20]

Here was a world turned upside down, where master accepted a secondary role and where slaves became the (temporary) social leaders, dressed often in the most amazing finery, mocking their betters and superiors and collectively thumbing their noses at the world which kept them servile. Of course it ended as quickly as it began; slaves slouched off to the fields, back to their chores as Christmas ended. The old order was instantly put back in place. It became clear to all that slavery was more easily managed and kept in place by allowing those occasional outbursts of enthusiasms – loud, musical, drunken (even on a Christian festival). Like Mardi Gras in Latin countries, the more outrageous pleasures of the Christmas season did more than indulge the slaves; they profited the slave owners. Some disliked the whole business. In the words of Frederick Douglass,

> These holidays serve as conductors, or safety valves, to carry off the rebellious spirit of enslaved humanity… The holidays are part and parcel of the gross fraud, wrong, and inhumanity of slavery…

It was, he thought, mere lubricant to the slave system – to persuade slaves to return to their tasks when their revelries were over.

> So, when the holidays ended, we staggered up from the filth of our wallowing, took a long breath, and marched to the field, feeling, upon the whole, rather glad to go…[21]

The specific festivals which highlighted the slaves' calendar of pleasures differed from one colony to another. But most drew on similar origins: on African pasts, on Christian dates and festivals, on ancient European traditions transplanted (and transmuted) on the far side of the Atlantic. The set girls, mummers, *JonKanoo*, the festivals of the Roses – all and more were merely the more dazzling forms of a remarkably diverse and ubiquitous attachment among the slaves to highly ritualized and communal pleasures. At times, to read accounts of those festivals is to be carried back to the collective pleasures of pre-modern Europe, to the Mardi Gras, to the Wakes and Hiring Fairs, to the Shrove Tuesday excesses tolerated with such apprehension by the propertied orders across the face of Western Europe. But it ought also to remind scholars of cultural habits in Africa.[22] The whole process illustrates the complexity of the cultural processes evolving in the slave colonies.

White observers of slave festivals were stunned by the effort (and cost) which slaves invested in their communal pleasures. It was a constant source of amazement that people who seemed to have so little zest for work, and who had so few material returns to show for their working lives, could, come the festivals, conjure forth the most elaborate of costumes and decorations and tap into a boundless energy for pleasures. Men and women who had to be cajoled, prodded and threatened to work apparently came alive in their free time. Time and again observers (including people who had spent their lives in the slave colonies) were taken aback by the sheer zest of slave pleasures. It raised (and raises) obvious questions. Where did the energy come from? And whence, too, came the economic wherewithal to create the material splendours of such festivals? In fact precisely the same points were made at the same time of plebeian pleasures in Europe. Listless, poor people came alive in time for their calendar of collective pleasures; they positively fizzed with energetic enjoyment, in sharp contrast to the lassitude which seemed to infect their daily labouring life.

There were other parallels too. Slaves, like European working people, made elaborate acknowledgements of thanks and appreciation to their masters/employers. Plantation slaves went out of their way to amuse, entertain and serenade their owners, often in exaggerated displays of thanks and deference which belied the underlying antagonisms. It was almost as if these effusive displays served to underline a different subtext; that here were excessive displays of appreciation by people with very little to be grateful for, proffered to people who were the very source and origins of their miseries. Sometimes of course such displays may have been genuine. More often however it was tongue in cheek. But men who stood in the way of such pleasures – slave owners who refused to allow customary free time and festivals, especially at Christmas – might expect trouble from the slaves.

When contemporaries – visitors and residents alike – looked at slave festivals, few doubted that they were gazing at something unique. It reminded outsiders of a host of things; to some it echoed similar pleasures at home, in Europe, while it reminded others, in its musical elaboration and excess, of African habits. But it was also unmistakably anchored in the calendar of the Christian year. From the late eighteenth century onwards, the coming of more aggressive, proselytizing churches set in train efforts to curb and restrain the more excessive aspects of slave festivals and there were periodic rumblings about the disturbances they caused in urban areas. But it was hard to see what to do about them. Short of taming the people, of civilizing them to other norms of social behaviour (a task undertaken most overtly by the churches), it was hard to see what could be done. And it was at this point that the slave experience parted company most obviously from the patterns which emerged in the early nineteenth century in Western Europe.

What brought the older, pre-modern pleasures of the common people to heel was that complex process of social discipline set in train by urban and industrial growth. Put at its simplest, it was impossible to enjoy the old pleasures (the excesses of Shrove Tuesday football for instance) in the restricted confines of developing urban areas. The old games and festivals, with their communal turbulence and incipient threats of violence, simply could not be tolerated in urban communities where law and order and the balance of social control was precarious. Thus it was that a mosaic of urban regulations emerged – national laws along with local regulations – which were governed by local agencies (Watch Committees) and enforced by that new nineteenth-century phenomenon, the police force. Very quickly, the pleasures of the common people were regulated and controlled. A simple incident will suffice to illustrate: in 1834 a small child in York was imprisoned for a week for playing cricket in the street. As more and more people found themselves living in an urban habitat (many of them engaged in strictly disciplined industrial enterprises) a new code of behaviour emerged from the complex interaction of urban regulation, the discipline of the workplace and, increasingly, from the sense of discipline which more and more people internalized. The games people played, by the late nineteenth century, were different from the popular pleasures of a century before. Basically, British people had come to enjoy themselves in more disciplined, rational ways: ways more appropriate to an urban habitat. The pleasures of the modern British people were, then, the collective pleasures of urban society. It is at this point that the usefulness of comparative studies begin to break down. Though slave pleasures show many resemblances to the world of pre-modern popular culture, comparison fails in that phase of industrial change which overtook Britain, and then Western Europe, from the early nineteenth century onwards.

Of course, the problems of disciplining a free labour force was of a different order from that of controlling slaves. Until 1838 the key determinant of slave discipline (despite amelioration) was of course that (often bloody) code of local laws, and the threat (and reality) of violence which formed the rock upon which slavery was built. What happened thereafter is, as yet, not fully understood or explained. What form of collective disciplines replaced the more arbitrary forces of planters and their systems? Obvious explanations – of new policing systems and the informal controls of churches and schools – can go only so far to help explain social discipline.

It seems relatively simple to assign the major slave festivals to a formal category of leisure, though even that presumes a great deal. Much more ambiguous is the question of leisure in the humdrum course of the slaves' daily lives. In societies where masters expected a great deal of the slaves' free time to be put to fruitful use, to the benefit of both master and slaves, it is hard to see how slaves' free time can readily be equated with leisure. Only in the sense that it was time at the slaves' own disposal does it to come close to leisure time. And even if we view it as a surrogate effort on behalf of the planters, it clearly yielded important benefits for the slaves. It was from those free hours, albeit at work in provision grounds or elsewhere, that slaves began that process of material accumulation which proved so transforming a force in the mature years of slavery.

No less elusive is the question of the relationship between slaves' free time, and the maintenance of the *status quo*. For years, historians have debated whether the tolerance of pre-modern popular culture – the *charivari,* Mardi Gras and Shrove Tuesday outbursts – was a crucial element in the maintenance of stable social relations. It was important, so the argument runs, to allow the common people to blow off steam, to turn the world upside down. How far could such an explanation apply to the world of slavery? In a world characterized by a fearsome panoply of physical punishments and restraints, it seems a mere marginal issue to concentrate on slaves' free time. Yet it is clear, as slavery evolved, that more and more free days *were* allowed, by convention, local usage and legislative regulation. There was, quite clearly, a coalescing of opinion on this issue: that free time was good for all concerned. Viewed from the slave owners' position this may simply have been a recognition of mutually beneficial arrangements; free time meant refreshment, a salutary degree of slave independence and a diminishing of slave owners' economic costs. Slave-grown food was a significant saving for the slave owner. Yet there is plenty of evidence that, in time, slave owners came to accept, and in places encourage, the useful and rational enjoyment of slaves' free time. What they *rarely* accepted, never came to terms with and refused to countenance with anything but unease and bad grace, was the crude bacchanalian, that mood of drunken abandon and sexual licence which they felt seemed to characterize so much of their slaves' free time.

It might be worth comparing slave owners in the Caribbean with the pioneers of 'rational recreation' who came to typify British urban politics and business from the mid-nineteenth onwards.[23] Local politicians and magnates were eager to encourage working people to enjoy themselves in ways which were refreshing, useful and self-improving. But, like the propertied everywhere, they frowned on the fleshier, more hedonistic forms of communal pleasures. They went out of their way, and invested a great deal of time and money, to promote 'rational recreations': music (choirs, bands, concerts), formal learning (libraries and reading rooms) wholesome physical recreations (codified team games) and the cultivation of personal and socially useful skills (allotments, gardens, etc.). Free time used in ways which were at once enjoyable and yet elevating, pleasurable but improving – for oneself, ones family and ones community – could always strike a chord of sympathy among men of substance in nineteenth-century Britain, and persuade them to dip into their pocket for assistance.

The planters for their part wanted their slaves, on their free days, to apply themselves to endeavours which were, at once, useful and perhaps pleasurable. There was, in the last generation of slavery and, later, in those years which saw the emergence of a free black peasantry, a positive desire to see the development of personal and communal qualities which would socialize the slaves towards more 'rational' behaviour. The stronger the attachment to hearth and home – and plot and garden – the less likely slaves would be to pursue the more frenzied pleasures which seemed, to planters and outsiders alike, to belong more to an African past that whites both feared and sought to eliminate. Free time – rationally used – was an important instrument in the socializing of slaves, in the acculturation of slaves to a discipline which wedded them ever further to the overall slave system. The ultimate labour discipline of slavery might, at its simplest, be the crude application of violence and corporal punishments. But at the other extreme, free time provided a lubricant for slavery itself. Like Mardi Gras, here was a form of recreational activity which served to integrate workers into the labouring system in ways they did not fully recognize. But slaves, like workers elsewhere, might subvert the system and convert it to their own ends, by imposing on it a style which was all their own.

Students of leisure have told us a number of interesting tales; colourful, imaginative and revealing. But the importance of their work lies at a deeper level than the mere narrative. The history of leisure takes us into the functioning of complex social systems, allowing us to see how they worked and how they changed. More than that, the history of leisure also provides an *entree* to the mentality of the people involved, on both sides of the recreational fence. Closer study of the history of slaves' leisure will surely yield similar returns.

Part II

BRITAIN AND SLAVERY

5 Black society and slavery in Britain

Though Africans had arrived in Britain from early times (we know of Africans in Britain's Roman legions), their numbers were insignificant. Africans found their way to Britain in numbers through early maritime contacts with West Africa, and via trading links with other Europeans maritime peoples. An Elizabethan Proclamation of 1601 ordered the expulsion of black settlers. But the subsequent development of trade to, and settlement of, the Caribbean ensured that their numbers would grow. Their arrival posed legal problems, (which mounted as their numbers increased) for slavery had long ago died out in England (though not so in Scotland). What was the legality of slavery in a country which, after the political upheavals of the seventeenth century revolution, prided itself on its political liberties? The issue was not fully resolved until the abolition of the slave trade in 1807.

Some Africans were imported direct to England from Africa (by the Royal African Company and other traders) but the majority came via the Americas. Some were brought for sale, but most, as far as we can tell, travelled to England with their owners: visiting or retiring planters and military and colonial officials. Crew on board slave ships occasionally imported slaves for personal use or for sale. Though the numbers were always small, the growth of the Atlantic trade in the late seventeenth and eighteenth centuries increased the movement of Africans and of blacks born in the Americas. The largest single settlement came in the wake of the American Revolution and the departure of the British military and officials. Even then, the total number remains imprecise; it was unlikely to have been more than 10,000 in the 1780s. But from first to last, the size of the black community created political controversy.

Most blacks in Britain were male, perhaps a reflection of the overall sexual imbalance in the Atlantic slave trade itself. Naturally enough, those men sought female company among women of their own humble social class. That too created social friction, or at least gave grounds for complaint from critics who were unhappy to contemplate the development of a black community in Britain. Yet it is not clear even if the term 'community' is appropriate for what emerged. The evidence suggests that only in London were blacks able to cohere into a community with any meaningful structure. Most were isolated one from another, living with their owners or employers, like other domestics, and rarely able to meet other blacks. But in London – home to the largest group – there were periodic black gatherings, social occasions and, eventually, black political activity.

Domestic service provided the most obvious form of employment for blacks in Britain. There were also substantial numbers who, like Olaudah Equiano, made a living at sea on Royal Navy and commercial vessels. Some emerged from humble domestic roles to secure a different, improved status. Ignatius Sancho, notably, became a shopkeeper in Westminster. Such men were unusual, yet both men are important for the way they illustrate a generally neglected (but important) aspect of local black life. Each had links to other blacks. Equiano in particular had black friends and associates across London, in North America and in the West Indies, visiting them on his voyages and receiving messages from them. Blacks in Britain were clearly part of a broader black community which reached from the slave barracoons of the African coast to the slave colonies of the Americas and on to Europe. All were linked by the enslaved experience of the diaspora. But there were obvious distinctions between the slave experience in Britain and the Americas. Could slavery simply be transplanted from the Americas into the metropolis?

Religion was a key issue. Planters in the British Caribbean had, from the early days, refused to admit African slaves to local (Protestant) churches. In slave-owning eyes, slaves were pagan brutes, beyond the pale of civilized life. In the words of the Barbados Assembly in 1681, the slaves' 'Savage Brutishness renders them wholly uncapable' of conversion to Christianity. Shortly after, the Jamaican Assembly took a more sympathetic line, urging the baptism of those slaves which planters 'can make sensible of a Deity and the Christian Faith.' But they were clear that baptism did *not* bestow freedom.[1] At the heart of this debate lay one of the basic justifications for African enslavement; that Africans were heathen, living outside the reach of Christian civilization, for whom slavery was no hardship or misery. Though it was a key issue in the development of chattel slavery in the Protestant Americas, it also had unforeseen consequences for Europe.

From the early arrival of Africans, their religion (or apparent lack of one), was a sensitive issue. The 1601 Elizabethan Proclamation, ordering the expulsion of early black settlers in Britain, was linked to their heathenism. Not only did they cause resentment, and consume local foodstuff, (at a time of shortage) but also,

> most of them are infidels, having no understanding of Christ or his Gospel.[2]

In the course of the eighteenth century, however, as more and more blacks arrived, many of those working as domestics in prosperous homes were converted and baptized. Parish records document black baptisms (and, of course, marriages and deaths). Black baptisms took place in all corners of Christian Britain, from the most humble and remote of local parish churches through to the nation's great cathedrals. The parish registers of Bedfordshire, for example, are dotted with black baptisms from the late seventeenth century onwards.[3] A similar story unfolded in York, the second centre of English Christendom. As early as 1687 a black ('John Moore the Blackamoore') was even made a freeman of the city of York – at a cost of £4.[4] In May 1777, Benjamin Moor, 'the son of James Moor, a Black Man living on Little River, north of Charles Town in South Carolina', was baptized in York Minster.[5] Later that same year, a seventeen to eighteen year old 'negro servant belonging to Mr Hutton' was also baptized in York Minster.28 Recent research on a clutch of London parishes, for the years 1780-1811, has revealed details of 159 black baptisms (the great majority of whom were young men).[6] In one case we know of in detail, Equiano the African had been nudged towards Christianity by sailors, by white domestics he had worked and lived with and by his employers.[7]

Black baptism was, then, unexceptional in eighteenth-century England. The critical question remains however; did baptism bestow freedom? Though a number of seventeenth-century legal cases had suggested that the `heathenism' of imported blacks confirmed their bondage, the West India lobby was particularly anxious to clarify the matter; they were unwilling to bring slaves to England if the slave could secure freedom by baptism (or even by stepping ashore in a free land). The matter seemed to have been decided by a ruling of law officers in 1729 – the famous Yorke-Talbot judgement. In reply to a petition from West Indian interests, the Attorney and Solicitor General asserted that slaves were *not* freed by simply landing in England. Moreover they ruled that

> baptism doth not bestow freedom on him, nor make any alteration in
> his temporal condition in these kingdoms.

This judgement was confirmed twenty years later by Yorke (now Lord Chancellor Hardwicke). Popular mythology however remained wedded to the idea that baptism conferred freedom.[8]

In 1762 Equiano was kidnapped, in London, and shipped back to American slavery. But he had here fallen victim to *English* slavery. It was not the slavery which thrived in the Americas (though that too had ensnared him earlier) but was a peculiar institution which existed in England itself. However vaunted the English pride in the freedoms secured in the revolution of the previous century, slavery clearly existed in England throughout the seventeenth and eighteenth centuries. And it was, as Equiano had so painfully discovered, a consequence of the Atlantic slave system.

On the eve of the European incursions into the Americas, slavery had declined across Europe. However, European settlers in the New World quickly evolved forms of slavery they had dismantled at home and some, notably black chattel slavery, they had never used.[9] Slavery in England had long since disappeared, but the rise of the slave colonies saw the transplantation of an alien slavery *back* into English (and British) life.[10] It was a simple – and inevitable – process, but its consequences were enormous. Men returned from a career in (or even a visit to) the slave colonies, in the company of enslaved domestics. Some vessels involved in slave trading (and there were some 11,000 of them in the course of the eighteenth century) returned to British waters with slaves on board. The numbers were always small (why bring costly slaves to Britain when they were more valued in the Americas?). In time however they came to form a noticeable presence, their numbers sometimes augmented by larger groups, notably after the British defeat in the American War in 1783 and the flight of loyalists and their slaves. Historians continue to argue about the numbers involved.[11] But there can be no dispute over the basic fact that for the best part of two centuries – perhaps even longer – black slaves were to be found in Britain.

Many were African, some of them brought direct from Africa, though most, like Equiano, arrived in England via the Americas. Others had been born in the slave colonies. Their story can be told via a number of historical sources, most revealingly perhaps the advertisements which dot contemporary prints and newspapers; advertising slave sales, seeking the return of runaways, or merely mentioning their existence in passing. Many of such notices appeared in the London press (understandably since both slavery and the press were more developed in the capital).

> A Negro boy about 12 years of age, that speaks English, is to be sold. Enquire of Mr Step (?) Rayner, a Watchmaker, at the sign of the Dial, without Bishopgate.[12]

Another advertisement offered for sale,

> A Black boy, twelve years of age, fit to wait on a gentleman, to be disposed of at Denis's Coffee House in Finch Lane, near the Royal Exchange.[13]

More starkly, in 1728 readers of the *Daily Journal* were told,

> To be sold, a negro boy aged eleven years. Enquire at the Virginia Coffee House in Threadneedle Street...[14]

Because a slave was property – part of the material estate of their owner – they were disposed of like other forms of goods and chattel. When John Rice was hanged for forgery at Tyburn in 1763, 'his effects were sold by auction, and among the rest his negro boy.'[15] Eight years later, the *Stamford Mercury* recorded that '...at a recent sale of a gentleman's effects at Richmond a negro boy was put up, and sold for £32.'[16]

Other major slave ports had their own (more modest) slave sales in the local press. In Liverpool, a local advertisement offered for sale,

> ... at George's Coffee House, betwixt the hours of six and eight o'clock, a very fine negro girl, about eight years of age; very healthy, and hath been some time from the coast.[17]

Occasionally we catch a detailed glimpse of British slaves (their physical appearance and characteristics) in ways which were rare for other plebeian peoples of the time simply because they *were* slaves. In Bristol in 1715, the local postmaster offered two guineas and expenses for the return of 'Captain Stephen Courtney's negro aged about 20 having three or four marks on each temple and the same on each cheek.'[18] A Scottish slave sale offered

> A NEGRO WOMAN, named Peggy, about nineteen years of age... speaks good English; an exceedingly good housewench, and washer and dresser; and is very tender and careful of children. She has a young child a NEGRO BOY, about a year old, which will be disposed of with the mother.[19]

Black slaves became so commonly available in Britain that in 1769 Catherine the Great sent an agent to purchase 'a number of the finest, best-made black boys, in order to be sent to St Petersburg, as attendants on her Russian Majesty.'[20]

This *ad hoc* process of small-scale black (mainly domestic) migration to Britain inevitably created legal problems. In English courts, local slavery confronted traditions which were contrary to the habits of the Americas. Perhaps the most important consequence of the seventeenth-century revolution was the defence of individual liberties guaranteed by the Habeas Corpus Act of 1679. Though designed for a different purpose, this Act was to have major implications for the history of slavery in England. But what did slaves, like Equiano, arriving in England know about the law? What practical help could they secure from a legal process which tended to support the interests of the slave-owning class? After all, the prosperity which flowed from the Atlantic slave system was plain for all to see. And slavery seemed indivisible; it was an Atlantic system which bound together three continents. When legal conflicts emerged it was soon clear to English judges that decisions about slavery in England could easily prove to be the solvent of the broader slave-based prosperity. Any decision which denounced slavery in England might have consequential effects on slavery in other parts of Britain's Atlantic empire.[21] Though English slave cases might seem particular – local – they could easily lead to an unravelling of the entire fabric of British Atlantic slavery.

There were, moreover, people who wanted slavery to thrive in England. The West India lobby for example sought to secure their hold over slaves in England by a variety of tactics. They actively publicized those legal pronouncements which supported their position and which confirmed the right to hold slaves in England. They sought to prevent black baptisms, if only because the popular belief that baptism conferred freedom simply refused to go away. But efforts to prevent the spread of black Christianity were counter-productive; they alienated outsiders and, in any case, failed to work.

Black slaves turned to the only practical way out. They ran away. It was of course impossible for Equiano to escape from re-enslavement in 1762. He was in that most vulnerable of positions – already on board a ship and with no direct access to friends or refuge on shore. Others were luckier. Again, we know about such runaways both from the legal consequences of their escapes, and from the regular newspaper advertisements seeking their return. In 1696 the *London Gazette* carried the following;

> Run away from Captain John Brooke of Barford near Salisbury, about the middle of August last, a middle-sized Negro Man, named Humphrey, aged about 30, in a dark brown Cloath Coat with hair Buttons...

In 1768, the *Liverpool Chronicle* advertised for the return of

> A Fine Negroe Boy, of about 4 feet 5 inches high. Of a sober, tractable, humane Disposition, Eleven or twelve Years of Age, talks English very well, and can Dress Hair in a tolerable way.[22]

But where could they run *to*? Some were lucky and found a comfortable refuge. Ignatius Sancho ran away from domestic work with domineering sisters and escaped to work in the more sympathetic household of the Duke of Montagu.[23] But other black fugitives clearly had greater trouble. Some must have stood out in a crowd, their physique, markings (especially those with African facial markings) and clothing making them hard to ignore.

> Run away from his Master about a Fortnight since, a lusty Negroe Boy about 18 years of Age, full of pockholes, had a Silver Collar about his Neck engrav'd Capt. Tho. Mitchel's Negroe, living in Griffiths Street in Shadwell.[24]

From the mid-1760s however runaways in London acquired an important defender. Granville Sharp was a man who both cared for their physical well-being, and who was keen to promote their claims to freedom both through the courts and among the politically influential. Sharp was to prove a critical figure in the history of English slavery. Later, Equiano and other Africans formed an important alliance with Sharp to defend black interests in England.

Sharp had discovered the plight of London's blacks by accident. Born in 1735 into a northern ecclesiastical family, Sharp had served his business apprenticeship in London before taking up a post in a government department. He was an industrious, serious young man, devoted to his Bible and his siblings, and who found pleasure in the family's weekend travels and in their collective music-making. But his life – and his subsequent reputation – were to change for ever in 1765. He bumped into a young black, Jonathan Strong, who had been severely beaten by his master David Lisle, a Barbadian planter. Sharp took the wounded man to his brother, a doctor, who tended him and supervised his recovered. Two years later, the erstwhile master met the now-healthy Strong, and promptly had him kidnapped and prepared for transportation to Barbados. When alerted, Sharp was galvanized into action, persuading a local magistrate to have Strong released.

It was a turning point for both men. Strong had – narrowly – avoided Equiano's fate of three years earlier in being shipped back to West Indian slavery, and Sharp resolved to press on with the defence of England's blacks.[25] Sharp's discussions with lawyers, however, revealed that English law might favour the slave owners, though there was an ambiguity which he resolved to exploit.

From 1767 onwards Sharp began to educate himself in the law, studying past cases, precedents and judgements in the search for the principle of universal freedom in England. His personal view, based on a close textual analysis of the law, was that the infamous 1729 York-Talbot judgement (that slavery was tolerated in England, and that slaves could be returned to the islands against their wishes) was legally flawed. He distributed copies of his argument among lawyers and this had the effect of dissuading Strong's putative owners from claiming damages against Sharp for having prised their slave from their possession. Jonathan Strong however did not enjoy his English liberty for long; he died a few years later aged only twenty-five.

Granville Sharp was now determined to clinch his argument and overthrow the York-Talbot judgement, to establish the general principle that enforced repatriation from England was illegal. Thus, in 1769 he published his major tract *A Representation of the Injustice and Dangerous Tendency of Tolerating Slavery: or of Admitting the Least Claim of Private Property in the Persons of Men, in England*. Were his argument to be accepted, the law would not tolerate slavery in England *or* the enforcement removal of people out of England. It was a principle which threatened the slave lobby, and indeed anyone who wished to employ or transport people as slaves. More than that, however, it formed the kernel of a more broadly based argument. It might only be a matter of time before the denunciation of slavery as an uncivilized, inhuman – and illegal – institution rippled outwards, from English usage and acceptance, to the slave colonies themselves. If slavery were immoral and illegal in England, what justification could be offered for slavery in Britain as a whole, or for the British slave trade; for the transportation of tens of thousands of Africans in British ships? Clearly, Sharp's intention were simpler and more limited – to protect threatened blacks in England. But the *consequences* of what he did were potentially enormous – and the West India lobby knew it.

Sharp effectively set in train a two-pronged defence of the black community in England. Firstly he offered them a legal defence, by establishing that English law was their defender, not their enemy. It was to take a whole generation before that battle was finally won, but Sharp's actions marked a break with a contrary tradition which stretched back more than a century, namely the use of English courts to give legal succour and comfort, not to the slaves, but to the slave owning lobby. Secondly, Granville Sharp offered practical comfort to blacks who found themselves threatened by arbitrary arrest and kidnapping. He and his growing band of friends were not of course always successful. What mattered however was that here was a man blacks *knew* they could turn to for practical assistance. Sharp's reputation soon spread. Not surprisingly, Equiano later knocked on Sharp's door when he needed a sympathetic English friend.

Blacks in London quickly learned that they a friend in Granville Sharp. One such was John Hylas, a free black whose wife Mary – still a slave – had been shipped back to Barbados against her (and John's) wishes in 1766. Sharp organized John's legal case against Mary's owners (who were ordered to return her and to pay John a derisory 1/- damages). Such cases however failed to deter slave owners from shipping blacks abroad. In 1770 Sharp was again called in, at the last moment, to prevent another former slave, Thomas Lewis, being brutalized and shipped back to Jamaica. It was a close run thing; the offending captain had sailed from Gravesend bound for the Downs, but contrary winds delayed departure, giving Sharp time to have a last minute writ of *habeas horpus* served on the captain. Sharp promptly took legal proceedings on behalf of Lewis, hoping to secure a general judgement which would prevent subsequent cases of kidnapping and transportation. The case came before Lord Chief Justice Mansfield in 1771; he was deeply reluctant to make so general a point of law that would outlaw such cases, and merely expressed the pious hope that

> I would have all the masters think them free, and all Negroes think they were not, because then they would both behave better.[26]

It was a hesitant performance by the Lord Chief Justice which angered Granville Sharp, who was now more than ever determined to clinch a lasting legal judgement on behalf of blacks in England.

Sharp's campaign came to a focus in the person of James Somerset, who had arrived in England from Boston to serve his Scottish master, Charles Stewart. Somerset had, like so many others, simply run away, only to be recaptured and imprisoned on the *Ann and Mary*, bound for Jamaica under Capt. John Knowles. A writ of *habeas corpus* was issued and the case began in February 1772. Angered by the actions of Lord Mansfield in the preliminary hearing, Sharp determined to mastermind the case, organizing and financing a sympathetic counsel, Francis Hargrave, who had already worked out a strong case against slavery in earlier discussions with Sharp. The case hinged, once again, on the contradictions in English law; did it, or did it not, sanction the enforced repatriation of blacks from England against their wishes? Mansfield, again reluctant as ever to be involved in a decision fraught with so many implications, tried to persuade the parties to settle the matter out of court. That, however, was precisely what Sharp did not want. What Sharp and his colleagues wanted was a clear-cut judgement.

The case moved through a number of hearings from February 1772 to early summer. Lord Mansfield regularly hinted at the consequences ('many thousands of pounds would be lost to the owners by setting them free'). Throughout, the outcome remained unclear, not least because of the Lord Chief Justice's prevarications. But as the case stumbled through various delays, it served to heighten public interest in the issue. When judgement was finally delivered, in June 1772, it took place before a packed Westminster Hall. Reporters from the capital's major newspapers, slave owners – and a large gathering of blacks – crowded the gallery. According to one report, a

> great number of Blacks were in Westminster Hall yesterday, to hear the determination of the cause, and went away greatly pleased. When Mansfield made his judgement, the blacks in the court, bowed with profound respect to the Judges, and shaking each other by the hand, congratulated themselves upon their recovery of the rights of human nature, and their happy lot that permitted them to breathe the free air of England...[27]

In fact, the air was not quite as free as they imagined. What Mansfield had determined was altogether more restricted a judgement. The Somerset Case ended only with the judgement that slaves could not be removed from England against their wishes. Mansfield had *not* resolved that slavery in England was illegal, though this last point was repeated in various newspaper reports and, more recently, by modern scholars. Slavery survived – legally – in England (though assailed by a changing political and social climate). But to remove slaves against their wishes *was* illegal. There remained of course the practicalities; how could a poor black, like Equiano in 1762, secure the necessary assistance and legal help when confronted by a swift and organized an effort at kidnapping? Their only hope lay in having a friend close by who might be able to raise the alarm and bring in suitable help. Equiano and others – how many we will never know – were unlucky.

The proof that Mansfield's judgement did not outlaw slavery in England lies in the mention of slaves and slavery existing *after* 1772. Slaves and slave cases periodically flitted in and out of the public gaze. Only two years after the Somerset Case, in 1774 , a woman sought charity from John Wilkes for herself and her baby, claiming '...that she was married to a black, who was a slave to a merchant in Lothbury...'.[28] Even in the last years of the century, by which time a pronounced abolitionist sentiment had transformed the political climate, local blacks were periodically kidnapped for transportation to the slave islands. In 1790 Hannah More told Horace Walpole the story of a terrified young black woman being dragged from a hiding place in Bristol and forced on board a ship bound for the West Indies. At the last minute, when the ship had to return to port, local Quakers secured her freedom. Hannah More confessed that, had she known about the incident in time, she would have raised money from among her friends to buy the girl's freedom.[29] Even when not enslaved or destined for the slave colonies, blacks long remained exposed to arbitrary arrest and maltreatment, exposed by their colour – and by the hostility to it – to whatever punishment seemed fit for their shortcomings. Occasionally, such kidnapping came to the public attention. Even then, the press reports often betrayed a sneering cynicism towards the aggrieved black.[30]

The ambiguity about slavery in England continued as late as 1827 – a full half-century after Mansfield's ruling in the Somerset Case. An appeal to London from a Vice-Admiralty case in Antigua (heard initially in 1826) concerned Grace Jones, a domestic slave who had voluntarily travelled with her mistress to and from England and who was seized by customs officials. The case hinged on the argument that the movement of a slave to and from Antigua contravened slave laws. Sitting in the High Court of Admiralty in London, Lord Stowell determined that Grace Jones had no claim to freedom,

> merely by having been in England, without manumission…

Stowell also worried, like Mansfield half a century before, that his ruling was fraught with commercial complications. There was a possibility that 'public inconvenience…might follow from an established opinion that negroes became totally free in consequence of a voyage to England.'[31] By then of course there was a mounting campaign in Britain against slavery and it was only a matter of time (and compensation) before slavery was abolished. Yet the critical issue was the legality of slavery *in England*. The case confirmed the right of West Indians to bring their slaves to, and remove them from, England.

There was however a distinction between the law and social practice. In the years after the Somerset Case, however specific its legal strictures, it is hard to find evidence of slavery in England. The examples we have are few – and were not on the scale (frequency or infamy) of the 1760s and 1770s. Something clearly had indeed changed. Yet these were the years when slavery in the British Caribbean reached its apogee. The years of the late eighteenth century saw the Caribbean disgorging slave-based prosperity as never before. Yet slavery in England seemed to fade away, driven into marginality not so much by legal decisions but by a changing social and political climate. One element in that changing climate was the work and influence of a small band of Africans, best remembered of whom was Olaudah Equiano.

In this new social climate slavery could no longer be easily sustained in Britain. Slaves ran away, or were targeted by free blacks and their white friends. Moreover the rapid rise of abolition sentiment had directed pressure on the Atlantic slave trade (which ultimately sustained the flow on blacks to Britain). Even as early as 1789 it was clear that the slave trade was doomed. Moreover, slaves were too valuable in the West Indies to be carried to Britain to be displayed as exotic domestic items in the social world of the prosperous. This decline in black migration was compounded by the seismic impact of the French Revolution and the subsequent wars. Yet, for the best part of two centuries, black slavery had existed in Britain, however small the numbers involved. It was just one more variant of that massive British slave system which sustained the development of the Atlantic world in the seventeenth and eighteenth centuries.

6 British abolitionism, 1787-1838

The British abolition movement was perhaps the most successful pressure group in modern parliamentary history. Within a mere twenty years of its initial foundation in 1787 the movement saw the end of the British Atlantic slave trade. Later, when the movement was reformed and revitalized (post-1825), British slavery itself was abolished. No abolitionist in 1787 would have dared to hope that the movement would succeed so quickly and so thoroughly. They were, however, aided by forces they could scarcely have understood or predicted. The abolitionist movement succeeded in large part through invisible forces currently transforming British life, in conjunction with seismic changes among the slaves in the colonies. The abolitionist movement has of course been praised and rewarded for bringing down the British slave system. It is not to deny its importance – nor to minimize its crucial contribution – to suggest that modern historians must look for a much broader explanation than parliamentary (or extra-parliamentary) histories for a satisfactory account of the end of the British slave system.

Firstly, it is important to understand why abolitionists have received so much praise. In the historiography of abolition, it was seductive, until 1945, to take abolitionists at their own face value. Throughout their political careers, the most prominent abolitionists (notably Thomas Clarkson and William Wilberforce) were great publicists, for themselves and their campaigns. Indeed it was part of their goal to establish in the British mind that they and their followers were the personification of the drive to end slavery. Theirs was also an era which saw the unfolding of history in personalized terms; history and contemporary affairs were largely the story of great personages locked in titanic struggles. This image, assiduously promoted by the powerful abolitionist propaganda machine, portrayed abolitionists as the good *versus* evil (slave owners). It proved an effective ploy. Moreover, after emancipation in 1838, it was an image that was perpetuated by successive generations of nineteenth-century historians and commentators, keen to describe abolition as a triumph of godly men against the forces of darkness.

For more than a century the story of abolition was typically portrayed as the triumph of good (and godliness) over evil. It would of course be difficult to deny the basic essence of that simplification without appearing to strip slavery of its gross immorality. And that, in a way, was the essence of the triumph of British abolitionists. What they did, quickly, unexpectedly and, in many respects, quite brilliantly, was to capture the high moral ground. They secured for themselves a position of unapproachable moral invincibility. Their posture seemed unimpeachable; they were godly men (and later, godly women) seeking to ensure

God's will was done, in a struggle which pitched them against a slave system which they castigated for its godlessness. Needless to say, the real story was much more complex than that. Yet it needs to be stressed that the triumph of abolitionism helped to establish its own interpretation as *the* explanation for the ending of British slavery. The mythology of abolition lived on to become part of the accepted canon of British historiography. In the years since 1945 however new views have prevailed.

The origins of the British abolition movement were rooted in the influence of Enlightenment writing (most notably Montesquieu) and the development of British nonconformity and evangelicalism. The majority of men in the first abolitionist group in 1787 were Quakers. And it was Quaker groups, which had been created across the face of Britain from the early eighteenth century, which gave the founding abolitionists an immediate national network. The movement knew that it had friends and sympathizers in most corners of the country. Thus, when speakers set out to address audiences throughout Britain, they had local sympathizers who provided a bed, organized a meeting place and could rally an audience. They were also – and crucially – a literate constituency. On the eve of the French Revolution, a national network of abolitionists had sprung up on the back of religious organizations. Moreover, many of the activists in the locality were influential; prominent men whose authority and status was unimpeachable and who could, accordingly, secure a respect and a hearing in their locality.

Abolitionists achieved this rapid development because they were remarkably well connected. London Quakers (on the eve of early abolition) had Friends and sympathetic contacts in most corners of the nation who were willing to provide help for speakers or to distribute publications. But they also caught a rising tide of literate political awareness, first noticed under Wilkes (and which was to become still more pronounced with the Corresponding Societies movement in the early 1790s).

The London Abolition committee, though theologically devout, consisted of practical businessmen who quickly appreciated the need for a national, popular campaign. In Thomas Clarkson they found the ideal peripatetic agent, ceaselessly spreading the abolitionist word (often at great risk to himself) throughout Britain. Abolition was above all else a brilliant propaganda campaign that used the printed word and a host of graphic and material images to broadcast the horrors of the slave trade. In a society already marked by the drift to urban life, with the early shift, in key areas, to industrial change (notably in Manchester) and with ever more people able to buy more and more material artefacts (notably of course the slave-grown products of distant empires), the British people were in a state of remarkable flux. They were prone to change and open to new ideas.[1]

Abolitionism was greatly aided, indirectly, by the loss of the American colonies in 1783. That national humiliation proved to be a catalyst which prompted a reappraisal of a host of British ideals and systems. The American break-away 'contributed to a revolution in the nature of radicalism in Britain.'[2] Moreover the radical debate in Britain which had swirled around the American revolution had been replete with the imagery of slavery. In a word, slavery itself had been politicized.[3] The London committee of 1787 was ideally placed. It had influential friends inside and outside Parliament (most notably of course William Wilberforce), it could rely on well-placed friends scattered throughout the country, and it was faced by a growing literate population (especially among the middle class) willing to hear a reforming message. Around the hard-working, plain-speaking person of Thomas Clarkson, anti-slavery was swiftly transformed from the preserve of a small band of metropolitan men of sensibility into the stuff of national popular politics.

The abolitionist groups which proliferated nationally were products of post-American War Britain. They spoke on issues, and with a political tone, which were unmistakably shaped by that war and by the loss of the colonies. That conflict had hinged on questions of representation, and confronted basic political principles. It also embraced a debate about liberty (in which the British had been seen as transgressors and the violators of traditional liberties). Anti-slavery provided the opportunity of elevating Britain by seizing the initiative and restoring the British belief that they, above all others, were a people wedded to liberty. After all, which institution seemed more violent and more thoroughly a denial of liberties than the Atlantic slave system?

To ever more people, slavery seemed both wrong and oddly old-fashioned; a throwback to a mode of conducting business (through a system of strict protection) and a fashion of dealing with mankind which sat uncomfortably with a rising attachment to progress and modernity. The abolitionist committees enabled the emergent provincial, urban middle classes to come together, and to speak up in favour of a reform which was itself congruent with their broader social and economic interests.[4] Abolition was, then, construed as a blow for progress against an outdated, backward-looking and cruel economic system. But perhaps the most remarkable aspect of the abolition campaign in the late 1780s and 1790s was its ability to embrace more than the newly vitalized propertied orders. Artisans and working men, a large number of women – traditionally beyond the political pale – even children (courtesy of the proliferation of children's abolitionist literature) – were rallied to the abolitionist banner. On the eve of the French Revolution, the social and political alliances forged by the anti-slave trade movement enabled the campaign to claim to be the most popular movement demanding major political change.

Demands for the abolition of the slave trade – the easiest, most practical *entree* to the wider problem of colonial slavery itself – were firmly lodged in Parliament (supported by a massive, national base) *before* the upheavals of 1789. The French Revolution changed everything of course. Initially, the simple weight and logic of the Revolution's basic ideology - the rights of man – gave abolition added impetus. But for many of the propertied classes, the issues began to blur. The links between black freedom and broader social rights – and the subsequent degeneration of the Revolution into factional violence – raised the serious spectre of levelling and of social unrest. This was especially pressing when the British debate was played out in the context of revived plebeian radicalism and the related onset of distress in 1792. It seemed dangerous to discuss major political change – including abolition – with the example of France to hand. The slave revolt in St Domingue confirmed the point.

Initially though, it appeared that the Revolution would inspire key British reformers to press ahead with their demands for change. Abolitionists for example were able to capitalize on the mood for reform by attracting remarkable numbers of signatures to abolitionist petitions which they submitted to Parliament. They issued cheap and plentiful tracts; simple publications which presented abolitionist arguments in direct, crisp format to a British readership which was (at least in towns and cities) much more widespread than the government feared. We cannot tell how many people read this abolitionist literature. But we do know that it was consumed, in taverns, coffee houses, private homes and public meeting places, by the million. There was, quite simply, an extraordinary flowering of cheap abolitionist (and radical) literature which fed a growing appetite among armies of British readers for the literature of reform.

Between 1787–1789 there was, then, an upsurge in interest in abolitionist arguments. The abolitionists' opponents – the West Indian planters, Atlantic merchants and bankers and those with interests closely tied to the slave empire – were clearly taken by surprise. For more than a century they had thrived unchallenged by questions of morality or economic utility because they brought such amazing prosperity to Britain. Few could deny the well-being which flowed into the Mother Country. The urban centres of that success – Glasgow, Bristol, Liverpool (and London of course) – the magnificent stately homes which grew from slave-based wealth, the fashions of London and Bath, so often linked to the profits of slavery: all this and more was confirmation of the value, the *unquestionability* – of the Atlantic slave system. The benefits of black slavery were undeniable. Whatever moral doubts may have existed, they remained the preserve of a minority. Moreover the incalculable suffering which the British slave empire had brought forth was to be seen far away: in Africa, on the Atlantic crossings and in the slave colonies. There were, of course, thousands of Britons who knew what slavery really meant, most notably those men who worked on the slave ships and in the slave colonies, or those military and government officials who spent part of their careers in the slave colonies. But they too stayed silent.

This simple point is basic. For more than a century and a half, from the founding of British Caribbean slavery, the British had enjoyed the expanding wealth of their slave colonies without troubling themselves too much about the inhumanities and immoralities which underpinned the system. After 1787 all that changed, quickly and unexpectedly. Firstly, the broadly based ideals of Enlightenment writing raised the morality of slavery. A small glimmer of doubt was revealed, in small circles of the educated and Quakers, about the inhumanity of the slave empire. 1789 transformed that doubt into a major and a growing objection. The ideals of the revolution transmuted concerns about slavery into a major debate about the justification for slavery. But this debate, furthered by a self-confident band of abolitionists, had still to face the massive obstacle of economic self-interest. The slave-lobby's case was simple and apparently irrefutable. The wealth which poured into Britain's major slave ports was huge and irreplaceable. Were the slave trade to end, it would bring the slave-based wealth of the Americas to a rapid conclusion. Abolish the slave trade, argued the West India lobby, and Britain would suffer massive economic loss. It was an argument which seemed unanswerable.

For their part, the abolitionists adopted a different tack after 1787. Their basic premise was that they could attack the slave system of the Caribbean by ending the Atlantic slave trade. If Africans were no longer available, the planters would have to rely on existing slave populations for their labour force in the islands, and the planters would be obliged to treat their slaves better. And if their treatment of slaves improved, the health of the population would improve, the slave population would flourish and, before long, a black peasantry would emerge which would provide a pool of free labour, rather than slave labour. It was, of course, a highly speculative venture. But its basic principle had the benefit of being specific and manageable. It was within the realms of possibility to persuade the British Parliament to make changes in the British shipping system across the Atlantic: to end the British slave trade.

By 1792, the abolitionists had securely lodged the issue of abolition inside Parliament. Thereafter it was subject to the whims and unpredictabilities of parliamentary moods and accidents. Indeed, had Wilberforce been a better manager of votes, it is very likely that Parliament would have passed abolition *before* 1807. Ultimately however what intervened, and confused the course of abolition, was the war between Britain and revolutionary France, the revolution in Haiti and the domestic attack on British radicalism. From 1792 onwards, a growing body of opinion, inside and outside Parliament, came to fear demands for change. Calls for change seemed to be influenced by France and change threatened to initiate the disasters that the French had experienced in St Domingue. The slaves themselves had begun to play an obvious and undeniable role in the debate about their own future. This proved to be the turning point in the story of British abolition.

Initially, British MPs – and the propertied bodies which supported them – recoiled from the very idea of discussing the end of the slave trade, because it seemed likely to threaten a reprise of events in Haiti. It seemed, they claimed, madness to debate abolition when, in the Caribbean, there was a convulsion among French slaves which threatened to prove contagious. Indeed, planters throughout the region were deeply alarmed about the spread of slave insurrection from one island to another. They worried about travel between the islands, and everyone watched with horror as Haiti devoured a whole British army. The simple outcome was an effective end to realistic prospects for ending the British slave trade for a decade. Ultimately it took the end of Pitt's regime and the brief period of peace between Britain and France before abolition made further headway.

The Revolution, inevitably, had major repercussions in French colonial possessions and thence in the British islands (where white elites were terrorized by fears of slave unrest). After 1791, the early sectional and racial bickering in St Domingue deteriorated into a major slave revolt. In the ensuing conflict the sugar economy was destroyed, along with the power and the very being of the local plantocracy. The British, keen to seize another lucrative sugar possession for themselves, dispatched an invasion force to St Domingue, but the slave armies – and tropical disease – destroyed the British just as they had destroyed the French. The eventual rise of an independent black republic – Haiti – seemed to confirm the West India lobby's worst fears and predictions. After 1792, the abolitionists could never fully convince waverers (even those sympathetic to ending the slave trade) that abolition would not lead to slave insurrection.[5]

The Revolution – and its dramatic results on the far side of the Atlantic – entombed abolition for a decade. Concepts of liberty rapidly passed into disrepute, even among men and women who had been firmly on their side before 1789. When abolition came – in 1806–1807 – it did so under a fresh administration and thanks to a switch in tactics used by William Wilberforce. By then it was a matter of parliamentary tactics and manoeuvrings. Yet, from 1792 onwards there was no doubting the basic mood of the British people about the slave trade. They had turned decisively against it, whatever its economic benefits, nudged in that direction by a powerful and subtle propaganda campaign able to harness the emergent forces of mass literacy and the power of new non-conformity (notably in urban communities). It was a mood which was of a piece with a growing interest in freedoms on a broader front, most notably the attachment to economic freedom among the middling orders. Such people saw their material future and well-being best advanced by economic and social freedoms. The restraints and restrictions of the old economic order seemed designed to hold them back. And slavery and the slave trade were perhaps the most blatant creations of Old Corruption; an economic system which, for all its material bounty, was rooted in an economic and political philosophy which seemed increasingly out of kilter with the changing mood of the last years of the eighteenth century. Though Adam Smith may have been the apostle of the new philosophy, it was shared, at a humbler, more self-interested level, by an alliance of middling ranks whose personal economic fortunes were best served by a greater freedom in the conduct of economic affairs. It was precisely these people who formed the bedrock of the abolitionist campaign up to 1792.

After abolition in 1807 the British embarked on a new crusade: to persuade the rest of the world to follow their own self-righteous lead. Having turned their back on the slave trade (though they had, in the course of the eighteenth century, become the most important practitioners of shipping Africans into the Americas) they sought to persuade others to follow their example. Invoking morality and Christianity – but using the power of the Royal Navy and the diplomatic muscle of the Foreign Office – the British set about imposing abolition on the rest of the Atlantic world. Needless to say, few people were impressed by this remarkable, almost St Paul-like conversion on the part of the British. Within a very short space of time, they had transformed themselves from Europe's pre-eminent slaving nation into the aggressive disciples of abolition.

At the end of the European wars, the British used the Congress meetings to promote the case for international abolition – with varying degrees of success. The power they were able to use, through their ships and their diplomacy, was to be a feature of British international relations for the rest of the nineteenth century. Abolition in effect became a prominent aspect of British foreign policy. In the eighteenth century, the British had been the major scourge of millions of Africans; in the nineteenth century, the British postured as the saviours of Africans (and other peoples) from the threat of enslavement. This international role caused intense irritation and grievance to other powers, most notably the French and Americans. The simple power of the British – buoyed up by expansive industrial wealth, reinforced by major international possessions and implemented by a pre-eminent navy – masqueraded as a pious mission to safeguard virtue against the threats of evil. Opponents were more likely to see it in simpler terms.

British self-interest was no longer served by the slave trade and it sought to promote new forms of economic well-being by the promotion of freedom. But it was of course a freedom which suited a broad range of British interests. Freedom meant free trade, free labour, the free movement of capital; in effect the freedom of an ascendant British economy to invest, exploit and control as best it could within the constraint of a new economic world system. Whereas the old slave empires had belonged, roughly, to the old theoretical structures of mercantilist protection – closed systems controlled as far as possible from the metropolitan heartlands (and all for their benefit) – the ideology of nineteenth-century British economic success demanded freedom. We know of course, that this economic ideal had strict limitations. Nonetheless, it stood in marked contrast to the dominant ethos of the previous century. Freedom, not slavery, was the *leitmotif* of British Atlantic trade and business in the nineteenth century.

There was a brief respite, after British abolition in 1807, and before abolitionists renewed their attack on slavery itself. The gap was understandable. Firstly, the war consumed all energies and diverted all demands for change. But, perhaps more important, it was essential to wait, to see what results were produced in the islands by the ending of the slave trade. By the early 1820s, when the first census returns from the slave islands had yielded their data (under the Registration Acts) it was clear that the slave population was in decline. This is exactly what planters had predicted. But it was merely a natural cycle, until those young slaves (children when abolition was passed) entered their childbearing years. From the mid-1820s the slave population began to pick up and grow, slowly but steadily. In the meantime, however, planters faced with a possible decline in their slave labour force began to reorganize their slave gangs. One result was that privileged slaves and those who might have expected improvements found themselves labouring in the fields. These reorganizations – necessary for their planters – served to create discontent among the slaves.

There were other powerful forces for change among the slaves. First and foremost they were converting rapidly, and universally in the British islands, to Christianity, notably to dissenting churches (Baptists and Methodists). With the end of the slave trade, more and more slaves were local-born; the Africans began to die out and were replaced by slaves born in the colonies. And ever more of them were Christian. This had dramatic results which were long-feared by planters but generally unexpected by the missionaries. In the years immediately after the ending of slavery, Victorians tended to see black freedom as a triumph for outraged Christianity. We do no need to go back to that position to recognize that the coming of Christianity made a qualitative change in the slaves' lives. For a start it gave slaves an ideological cohesion which they had previously lacked. More than that, it gave them a direct bond with a growing band of abolitionists in Britain. In the past, the persecution of slaves had been seen as a means of keeping 'uncivilized' Africans in their place. But the punishment of Christian slaves was seen as unnecessary and cruel persecution of black Christians. Nonconformists in Britain were outraged to hear stories about the punishments inflicted on their black co-religionists. Thus, in an unusual twist, black and white came together as never before.

It was in the islands however that black Christianity produced its most fundamental changes. Firstly, the new chapels provided slaves with a meeting place away from the plantations. It also offered a forum for the emergence of powerful black preachers, steeped in the imagery and vernacular of the Bible. Men of charisma, powerful in presence and influence, emerged as leaders of local black communities. They spoke to their black following of the promises of a better life to come, of redemption, salvation and the Promised Land. They told of the crossing of the Jordan, of escaping from the house of bondage. All these images spoke directly to the slaves. The Old Testament in particular was replete with imagery with direct relevance for people in bondage, awaiting salvation and freedom. Visitors to the islands were deeply impressed by black Christianity – by its fervour, its noise, its enthusiasms. But its most impressive impact remained unnoticed at first, for it was crucially important in focusing slave attention on their condition, and raising their hopes of salvation to come.

Black church leaders demanded a salvation in the here-and-now. More and more slaves were unprepared to wait for the distant prospects of heavenly salvation. This demand, felt in different degrees throughout the islands, erupted in various forms. But its most potent expression took the form of the major slave rebellions: in Barbados in 1816, Demerara in 1823 and then, most brutal of all, Jamaica in 1831-32. The causes of each were local of course. But each was overlaid by the forces already mentioned: the restructuring of slave populations (and the frustration of slave expectations) and the rallying and ideological impact of Christianity. Running like a descant through it all was a rising sense of unease, in Britain, about the processes needed to keep slavery in place. Each slave revolt was suppressed with levels of violence that shocked metropolitan opinion. What had been unquestioned in the seventeenth and eighteenth centuries was now a matter of outraged concern. The British had become queasy about using collective killings, torture and destruction as a tool for maintaining their slave colonies. The question was asked; if slavery could only be kept in place by levels of violence on a truly medieval level, was slavery worth it? And here we touch on the other crucial element in the fluctuating story of British abolition. Britain itself was changing.

By the mid-1820s Britain was well into the process of major urbanization and industrial growth. A growing proportion of the people found themselves living in an urban habitat, areas which were more easily organized politically, and where the printed word could circulate more freely and readily. Popular literature swirled through British towns as never before. And abolitionists seized on the opportunity to saturate the country with their free literature. Millions of tracts and pamphlets promoting black freedom fluttered down on the reading public from the offices of local abolitionists. For those who were interested, there were regular lectures on the abolitionist circuits. Tens of thousands turned up to listen to the abolitionist case. Indeed the only restraint on abolitionist lectures was the physical capacity of the meeting places. In all this women played an increasingly notable role. Thus, the printed and the spoken word swept up the British people in a clever abolitionist movement.

Abolitionists from 1825 returned to the petition as an expression of opinion. Thousands of petitions, signed by millions of people, descended on Parliament, demanding first of all improvements in slavery and then a complete abolition. MPs were lobbied in their constituencies; they were in effect warned that unless they supported abolition in Parliament, the abolitionists would direct their powerful armies of supporters against the MP in any future election. Thus, a groundswell of abolitionist sentiment was built up, in the country at large and within Parliament. The whole process was completed in 1832 by the reform of Parliament. Though it inaugurated a far from democratic system, parliamentary reform swept away many of the old pro-slavery MPs, replacing them with men in favour of abolition. The abolition campaign had yielded good returns in its attention to constituency politics.

Thus, after 1832, it was but a matter of time before the British Parliament decided to end black slavery, which was disliked at home, disliked in Parliament and, of course, hated by its victims throughout the slave islands. Nor was it merely coincidental that Britain ended slavery at the moment it found its broader economic interests switching. Though industrialization was still embryonic in 1834, the shift towards a new world view which underpinned that process was already well advanced. By the late eighteenth century it was clear to more and more commentators (most notably Adam Smith) that the restraints on trade necessary to the old slave empire were ultimately damaging. The argument took a different form among those small-time investors and speculators who – for all the fabulous wealth normally associated with slavery – were the typical backers of the slave system. Men and women with spare cash to invest found that profits were higher – and certainly less speculative – in building houses or investing in local business at home, rather than sinking their money in ships and slaves. It was not so much that slavery became unprofitable. Rather that other forms of economic activity were more attractive, less risky and more easily controlled.

Parliament brought slavery to an end – partially – in 1834. It was terminated fully in 1838 throughout British colonies. Thereafter, the British made their abolitionist political instincts (replete with economic self-interest and diplomatic advantages) a major policy in the armoury of foreign policy. Abolition became a key factor in that cultural imperialism which became the hallmark of the British for a century and more. And it is worth recalling that the Anti-Slavery Society functions to this day from its London HQ.

The temptation of modern scholars is to see the abolition of the British slave system as merely a function of broadly based economic and social changes in Britain and the Caribbean. In part this is a healthy antidote to an older school which thought in terms of personalities and religion. Yet there has been a danger, in recent years, of relegating the abolitionist movement – and its prominent leaders. In truth they played a crucial role, for they were the catalyst which capitalized on those changes, often unconsciously. It was, after all, Parliament which abolished the slave trade and slavery. And we need to know how and why that political change took place. The difficulty facing future historians is to explain the precise mix – the exact juncture – between the specifically political, and the broad economic generalities. Though it seems doubtful that any future study will revert to an explanatory focus on the abolitionists themselves, it would be wrong to marginalize them.

7 Feeling superior: abolition and after

The granting of freedom to Britain's 750,000 slaves in 1838 was a defining moment, not merely for the ex-slaves but for the British themselves. It was to prove a crucial event in the development of a national cultural identity, and was basic to the British sense of themselves in their dealings with the outside world through the rest of the century. Emancipation was construed as a selfless act of humanity; a granting of freedom to legions of ex-slaves which stood as a symbol of Britain's love of freedom. It was *the* most significant assertion of Britain's attachment to the concept of freedom. The belief that the British were uniquely – even divinely – qualified to promote freedom flowed however not solely from the campaign against slavery, but traced its roots back to that titanic clash which spanned a generation, between Britain and the French. In the confused debate which swirled back and forth in the years of revolutionary ferment after 1789, the rhetoric and vocabulary of freedom was central.

There was of course a much older debate about freedom, reaching back to the revolution of the seventeenth century and to the events of 1776-1783. But the heightened tensions of 1789 re-ignited the debate. Under the shadow of the French Revolution, the debate was quickly polarized: minority, lower-class radicals on the one side, versus propertied orders on the other. Both sides however couched their political ambitions in terms of traditional freedoms. The Paineite claims of the 'Freeborn Englishman' locked horns with a Burkeian defence of the old order. The 1790s were years of deep divide and uncertainty, when the nation itself seemed threatened by the unstoppable power of French arms and the solvent of domestic radicalism. Eventually however, the debate about freedom was subsumed within a necessary upsurge of patriotism. War transformed everything. To win the war against France demanded a united national front: a front which claimed patriotism and freedom as its unifying emblem.

The British believed that the French wars had been fought (and eventually won) in the name of freedom. British freedom triumphed over aggressive French despotism, and Britons had united in destroying French militarism. This perception of national unity was, to a marked degree, flawed. In reality the fissures in British life were unmistakable, but they were kept carefully in check, and did not become obvious again until the years of social and economic dislocation after 1815. For more than a generation (1793-1815), the British had been organized for war, on an all-consuming scale, and with a single-mindedness which was not to be repeated until 1914-18, around a national commitment to freedom.[1]

The language and imagery of freedom in those years are there for all to see. Newspapers, prints, cartoons and iconography of all kinds bear public testimony to the ideological foundations of the French wars. Time and again, they address the question; freedom against invasion, freedom to remove foreign conquerors, freedom to defend a political system which was, the British claimed, the envy of the world. The war was more easily fought because the British were a freedom-loving people. Although it is easy to dismiss such claims as propaganda, the British came to believe it. Above all other people, they believed themselves be blessed by an attachment to the assertion of freedom.

There was of course an irony here, and one not lost on those bands of radical and reformers who argued for different kinds of freedom; for working people and for subject peoples. It was, in essence, the prototype of a debate which was to flourish many years later, in a very different British Empire. How could the British argue, and fight, for freedom while denying the same experiences to millions of their subject peoples?

The debate about freedom between 1789 and 1838 became basic in the shaping of a British cultural identity. Stated crudely, when Victoria ascended the throne in 1837, it had become a matter of great national pride that the British had girded up their loins and, within a few years, had overthrown French tyranny *and* then destroyed the slave empire. This conjunction of events is important. Although the campaign against the slave trade was initially obstructed by fears generated by the French Revolution, in time the vocabulary of abolition blended neatly with the language of freedom which was itself the vernacular of the French wars. Here were two struggles which pitched the lovers of freedom – the British – against forces of oppression. In a political war which liked to present complex issues as simple ethical alternatives, the British had triumphed over the forces of darkness.

The sense of national and cultural identity in existence by the early nineteenth century was that of a British people whose attachment to freedom had been shaped by a total war and tempered by a crusade against slavery. Looking back from 1838, the British found plenty of reasons to feel pleased with their efforts. Having secured the freedom of Europe from French aggression, they had recently freed their slaves. They contrasted the actions of their statesmen with the gory achievements of Napoleon. Wilberforce, said Samuel Romilly, saved 'so many of his fellow creatures', while Napoleon was wading 'through slaughter and oppression.'[2] Thereafter the British embarked on ensuring that others were not denied their freedom by being sold into slavery in the Americas; hence the Atlantic anti-slave-trade patrols by the Royal Navy.

The British were henceforth strengthened to embark on a crusade which would bring freedom to other deprived peoples. Such a crusade would, of course, have the added advantage of helping to secure Britain's wider economic well-being, in Africa or elsewhere. For here was the crux of the matter. As much as they persuaded themselves (and tried – less successfully – to persuade others) of the altruism of their global crusade for freedom, the British had a clutch of economic irons in the fire. Their rivals, notably the French and the Americans, could see the formula; that freedom, and especially certain kinds of free trade, were perfectly congruent with British economic interests. The British attachment to freedom, for all its high-flown principles, yielded obvious material benefits to Britain.[3]

The British economy – industrializing, serving an increasingly urban population, unable now to feed itself from local resources – needed to look to all corners of the world; for raw materials, foodstuffs, markets, in short for whatever commercial opportunities presented themselves. The restrictions of the old empire were gradually cast aside; most notable among them was slavery. At home and abroad, freedom to trade, to import and to sell went hand-in-hand with a freedom in the management of labour.[4] It was as if the material benefits of freedom had confirmed the older struggles for political freedom. If the years before 1838 had been couched as a struggle for political freedom, the years thereafter saw attention switch to economic matters. The Victorian economy began to flourish in an ideological atmosphere of freedom.

A growing number of economic historians now accept that, for all the contemporary bravado about matters of freedom as basic ingredients in the making of Victorian freedom, the loosening of restraints was indeed crucial in transforming the economy. Yet the century before had been no less vital in the development of steady economic growth. It seems clear enough now that the controlled mercantilist state and empire of the eighteenth century laid the basis for much that followed. What many have taken to be profligate expenditure on military forces in fact secured the British conditions for economic growth and rising domestic well-being.[5] The great wars of the eighteenth century not only maintained British dominance and expanded the British empire, but may even have paid for themselves. In the long run, no major power emerged to challenge British economic hegemony until the rise of the USA in the nineteenth century.

It made perfect sense in 1838 to speak of freedom as a key British cultural characteristic because it seemed to speak to the British political experience of the past half-century, and had also pointed the way forward to enhanced economic prosperity. On the basis of freedom, the British had maintained their own national security and had bestowed the same on others. In the name of freedom they could now advance, through trade and informal empire, to scarcely imagined levels of well-being.

The British campaign to end their own slave empire had taken a half-century. But when the 750,000 West Indian slaves celebrated full freedom at midnight on 1 August 1838, it did not mark the end of the British anti-slavery campaign. Indeed British abolition had developed a political and organizational momentum. There was formed a crusade by an indignant and pious people, organized and prepared to tackle slavery wherever it existed. Other nations saw the matter differently. The French, still conscious of the wounds inflicted by the British in the recent wars, were in no mood to accede to British diplomatic calls for international abolition. Indeed the British abolitionists' efforts to win over the French to black freedom may have been counter-productive, and the French only ended their own slave systems in the revolutionary confusions of 1848.[6]

The biggest challenge to British anti-slavery was, of course, the USA. A great deal of British political effort, money and moral and religious fervour was invested in campaigns to persuade the USA to abandon slavery. Publications and speakers criss-crossed the Atlantic; sister churches hummed with moral indignation. But there were powerful political and popular antipathies to British abolitionist efforts. The US had not gone its own way in 1776 simply to defer to British moral posturing. And like the French before them, there were Americans who pointed to the hypocrisy of the British poacher turned international gamekeeper; the pre-eminent eighteenth-century slave trader now masquerading as guardian of the world's morality. To American ears, British calls for slave freedom had a hollow ring, coming as they did from the nation which had conceded American liberty in 1783 only at the point of a gun. For all their efforts at home, and however influential the tactical example of their earlier campaign, British abolition ultimately remained marginal to the domestic American debate about slavery and freedom.

Other regions seemed more amenable to British persuasion, if only because they were directly under British control or influence. But here the British faced a different moral dilemma. Indian slavery for instance, unlike black chattel slavery in the Americas, owed nothing to European lineage. It was indigenous and rooted in social structures and customs which the British had barely begun to understand (still less appreciate). Yet slavery in India seemed ubiquitous, massive (involving perhaps as many as 16 million people) and proffered a number of offensive forms to British evangelicalism. To attack Indian slavery, as the British did from the 1830s onwards, was to confront Indian cultures head-on. This was an utterly different challenge from ending slavery in the Caribbean.

The British onslaught on Indian cultures was set back by the uprisings of 1857. British confidence that they might be able to recast the subcontinent in their own image was abruptly undermined. The more ambitious and aggressive of missionaries were henceforth kept in check, and the post-1857 political arrangements went out of their way to avoid alienating local peoples by trespassing on their customs. Victoria's Proclamation of 1858 stated the case boldly. The British renounced 'the right and desire to impose Our convictions on any of Our subjects.' Henceforth the greatest efforts went into bringing material improvement; 'the importation of the body of the west without its soul.'[7] In India at least it had become clear enough that the export of British freedoms was more difficult than many had hoped.

There were however other regions of the globe where British abolitionist activity might yield better results. Islamic slave trades for example continued to flourish. And slavery thrived in Africa itself. It is now clear enough, whatever the statistical uncertainties, that there was a dramatic increase in slavery *within* Africa in the wake of the ending of the Atlantic slave trade. Slaves were being moved in large numbers within Africa. Indeed it was these enslaved movements which Europeans encountered when they began those explorations of the African interior in the second half of the nineteenth century.[8] While the British congratulated themselves on the effectiveness of their Atlantic anti-slaving policies, African slaves continued to be scattered from their homelands. Perhaps three millions were moved to Islamic regions in the nineteenth century. British ships continued their anti-slave trade patrols off East Africa until the end of the century. In fact British vessels continued to stop dhows to examine them for slaves as late as the 1920s.[9]

The British were however as interested in events *within* Africa as they were in the enforced migrations of Africans overseas. They developed a remarkable curiosity for news about Africa, and much of what they heard served to confirm their aggressively evangelical instincts. Stories about the continuing horrors of slavery in and from Africa were given added strength from the mid-century by reports of missionaries. Whatever we may think of their aims, and their results, the missionaries relayed stories back to British congregations which helped keep alive the British commitment to anti-slavery. The urge to convert Africans had to confront many of the moral and tactical problems posed by the earlier cultural conflicts in India. How could the British and other Europeans disentangle and destroy cultural habits they disliked without allowing the whole fabric of local society to unravel? Whatever the problems, and however successful their efforts, the missionaries' stories from and about Africa became the stuff of vivid fantasy and widespread curiosity in Britain.

Few today would accept the image of Victorian missionaries so beloved of contemporaries. Like abolitionists up to the 1830s, the missionaries from the mid-century onwards tapped into a highly sensitized public interest which is hard to imagine today. The British public wanted their missionary heroes to be British – to be manly and tough, Christian and persevering in the Lord's cause. But, once again, the context is crucial.

Britain had changed enormously, both in its physical environment and cultural outlook. A majority of Britons now lived in urban areas where, among other things, the printed word was easily available. The British, with the obvious exceptions across the social divides, were now a literate people, keen on the printed word which flew at them in ever-increasing volume and forms. There were few groups or specialist interests which did not promote themselves through print; from local political radicals through to the local church. Cheap newspapers, magazines, comics and children's literature of all kinds completed the circle. From the earliest days of childhood literacy through to old age, the pleasures of reading were catered for. Time and again, with a minority, critical voice, there was a genre of literature which was steeped in the heroics of empire.

So many older people are familiar with this tradition from their own childhood reading, for instance, that it seems unremarkable. But we need to remind ourselves of the newness and the potency of that literature. Cheap, imaginative, ever changing, the popular literature of mid- and late Victorian Britain spawned a culture which paid inordinate attention to issues of empire and exploration. Best remembered in boys' adventure stories, this interest spilled beyond the realms of story-telling into the business of cult-creation.[10]

The popular cult of the Victorian missionary – especially after the death of David Livingstone – reflected precisely the national sense of moral and religious superiority. The apparent selflessness of armies of young missionaries, working in the most benighted corners of the globe, confirmed to the British a truth they took to be self-evident: that in the process of establishing themselves as the pre-eminent imperial power, they had secured a reputation of unimpeachable moral integrity. In the years after slave emancipation, this sense of superiority provided, in Linda Colley's words,

> irrefutable proof that British power was founded on religion, on freedom and on moral calibre, not just on a superior stock of armaments and capital.[11]

What has become clearer in recent years, thanks to research on the nature of British abolitionism to 1838, is the complex aftermath of the abolition efforts. Firstly, the campaign itself had politicized millions of Britons, notably women and working people, to a degree which no one had planned, and whose consequences none could predict. It was a process of politicization which fed into subsequent reform movements and provided a model for others to emulate. Subsequent reforming and pressure groups looked to abolition as a model of how to campaign – and a model of what could be achieved. At a different level, abolitionism gave the governing orders a powerful weapon in their dealings with the outside world. The British, the destroyers of black slavery in the British West Indies, now claimed to be 'the arbiters of the civilized and uncivilized world'.[12] It was, however, a mission in which, again, moral superiority rested comfortably with commercial self-interest. Take for example the comment of Lord Palmerston in 1842:

> Let no man imagine that those treaties for the suppression of the slave trade are valuable only as being calculated to promote the great interests of humanity, and as tending to rid mankind of a foul and detestable crime. Such was indeed their great object and their chief merit. But in this case as in many others, virtue carries its own reward; and if the nations of the world could extirpate this abominable traffic, and if the vast population of Africa could by that means be left free to betake themselves to peaceful and innocent trade, the greatest commercial benefit would accrue, not to England only but to every civilized nation which engages in maritime commerce. The slave trade treaties therefore are indirectly treaties for the encouragement of commerce.[13]

It was as if the circle had been completed. Africans were now viewed as producers and consumers, not as the raw material for American plantations. This is precisely what Equiano had argued in the 1790s.

Time and again, British statesmen adopted a simple line. They saw themselves as the inheritors of an abolitionist moral obligation which it was their duty to impose on the rest of the world. Informed of atrocities in Zanzibar, Palmerston wrote to the British consul in 1846, urging him to 'take every opportunity of impressing upon the Arabs that the nations of Europe are destined to put an end to the African slave trade and that Great Britain is the main instrument in the hands of Providence for the accomplishment of this purpose.'[14]

It was not quite the case that God was British, but rather that the British were uniquely blessed to carry out His work. And basic to that work was the securing of freedom around the world. To secure that freedom, the British had to confront and destroy various forms of slavery. After 1838 this was not simply a prompt from abolitionist pressure groups, for abolition sentiment had permeated to the heart of British politics and government.

For the governing order, this crusade after 1838 had the advantage of being remarkably popular. They were thus able to capitalize on the continuing groundswell of public abolitionist sentiment, which was itself sustained by anti-slavery organizations and publications. But from the mid-century this spilled over into a much broader public attachment to freedom as a cultural export. Statesmen *knew* that public opinion was behind them. Indeed, the campaign up to 1838 had been propelled by popular support to a degree that many involved found uncomfortable.

Yet even here, there was a hidden political benefit. The concentration on distant problems distracted attention from more pressing, domestic difficulties. This, after all, was a source of great irritation to those radical leaders who complained over a number of years of the way anti-slavery could achieve this deflection, though the hunger, frustration and simple explosion of plebeian anger, most notably in the Chartist outbursts in the 1830s and 1840s, were too strong and aggressive to be deflected by the tales of horrors done to slaves.

On the whole, however, the British abolition campaign had the effect of securing the attachment of millions to the political culture of their homeland. For the really hungry and desperate, this was scarcely enough. But there were many others, measured in their millions, whose loyalty and sense of identity was shaped and refined by anti-slavery. No other campaign attracted such numbers, accumulated so many names to its side, commanded such space in print, built up such parliamentary support, and commanded such public backing as the campaign against slavery. Anti-slavery had become a defining element in being British; a proof of the distinctive and divinely inspired qualities of the British people. And all this at a time when other peoples hesitated. The Americans continued to rely on and benefit from slavery, the French dragged their feet on abolition, and large parts of the Americas struggled to preserve their own forms of slavery. Who else in the West could compare with the British in their forthright and aggressive pursuit of freedom?

British abolition did not then come to an end with the emancipation of British slaves. There were slave systems in abundance the world over which demanded their attention. The era between the ending of the British slave empire and the apogee of a new form of British imperialism was neatly spanned by the reign of Queen Victoria, a monarch who came to personify British overseas expansion, her name scattered and appended to distant parts of the globe.

Though the later years of Victoria's reign marked the high-water line of the tide of British imperial sentiment, that phenomenon cannot be explained purely in material or military terms. Obviously it was fuelled by an expansionist economy yearning for markets and materials, and was secured by a relatively unchallenged military (especially naval) power. But it was also rooted in an ideology of empire which, in that new age of mass literacy, cheap print, public education and new popular cultures, quickly penetrated to the very grass roots of British life. Notwithstanding the critique of imperialism which formed a descant to the whole process, the British became a fiercely imperial people, from top to bottom. Imperial victories were celebrated, setbacks mourned, in the most collective and public of fashions. Nor was this simply a matter of the organs of the state whipping up imperial theatre. Wherever we look at British popular culture in the last twenty years of the nineteenth century, there we will find an enthusiastic and often belligerent imperialism. Indeed to be imperialist was to be patriotic; and patriotism was one of the most marked inventions of the nineteenth century, to be placed alongside the other great British inventions in those years (though like other inventions it too was based on earlier models).[15]

One example will illustrate the point. In that major forum for popular culture, the music hall, a place was regularly found for that remarkable song 'Rule Britannia'. Though written in the 1740s to commemorate the accession of the Hanoverians, the song came into its own in Victoria's reign. In the process its words were changed, by popular usage. Initially the song asserted, `Britannia, rule the waves', an injunction, not a description. A century later, when it had become a popular song, the contemporary format had subtly changed: `Britannia rules the waves'. The injunction of the eighteenth century had become the simple description of the nineteenth century. In the course of the nineteenth century, dozens of arrangements of the song were published, for instruments, orchestras and for voice, all part of that broader drive to satisfy the voracious British appetite for printed music, much of which was inspiring and patriotic.[16]

Perhaps the most curious aspect of `Rule Britannia' was the line, `Britons never will be slaves'. Here was a statement which was intended to be merely a rousing finale to a song (whose popularity the composer could never have imagined) but which, in fact, stands as a *leitmotif* to Britain's dealings with the outside world. At the time the song was written the British had established themselves as the most prominent and aggressive of the slave traders in the Atlantic economy. But when the song reached its peak of popularity, the British had transmuted themselves into the zealous and equally aggressive advocates of abolition and freedom. Here was a verse, almost a national anthem, which seemed ideally suited to Britain's new (self-appointed) global role as scourge of the slave trade and guardian of the world's liberties.

The British trumpeted their intention of safeguarding freedom on a global scale; itself a sign of their remarkable self-confidence, if not always their political grasp. Naturally enough it proved to be a complex, up-hill struggle, especially in their dealings with indigenous peoples in India, Africa and Arabia. But, in public at least, British statesmen and a host of pressure groups, remained steadfast in their attachment to the concept of freedom as an instrument of British colonial and foreign policy. Inevitably of course, things were not as simple as many believed.

There were difficulties at every turn. The first task the British set themselves was apparently the easiest; to seal off the routes from Africa and to staunch the flow of people which had provided the muscle for the development of the Americas. Looking at a map in London, the problem seemed manageable. With a Slave Trade department in the Foreign Office, and an anti-slave trade squadron in the Royal Navy, the British clearly meant business, notwithstanding the inevitable friction with other Atlantic maritime powers. As we know the British (and others) were unable to staunch that flow completely. It was sixty years before their efforts were counted successful, and even then at a cost of £40 million (seizing in the process 1600 ships and some 150,000 Africans.) It was, by any standards, a massive expenditure of time, money, resources and will power; indication enough of the early Victorian commitment to anti-slavery.

Few voices were raised against the idea that the British should direct their moral crusade in favour of freedom on a global scale. Critics were generally dismissed in what was an emergent consensus that the British had a `calling'; a divine mandate which demanded action, and which would brook no interference from other earthly powers. When British imperialists looked back to earlier empires, they liked to point to the Roman empire in the Age of Constantine; a Christian evangelical empire which imposed its orthodoxy across Europe. After all, it was the Roman empire which had abolished slavery in England. Directly or indirectly, imperial conquest could be used to advance a moral position. The British did not however need to look back for justification for their new imperialism. It was seen as a God-given imperative.

It is easy, now, to see how this view, so assiduously promoted in everything from children's books to serious newspapers, was central to that `culture of complacency' which underpinned the British view of themselves, and shaped their dealings with the wider world.[17] It was a culture which also had fundamental domestic consequences because it played a major role in undermining the resolve to tackle domestic matters. Problems at home could be passed off as mere blemishes when attention was drawn to the grander view of Britain's moral worldwide crusade. Of course, it was no comfort to Britain's wretched, growing in number, density and despair, to learn that the blessings of British freedom were currently being lavishly sprinkled round the world. The contrast between imperial grandeur and colonial paternalism on the one hand, and domestic squalor on the other, was not fully articulated until late in the century, and did not gain full political direction until the disaster of the South African war. True, there had been a persistent tradition of complaint (Dickens's telescopic philanthropy) but it had made little headway against that self-confident, British identity shaped by the collective attachment to freedom and the antipathy to slavery.

In most of the literature about the ending of British slavery, pride of place has traditionally gone, rightly, to the results of emancipation for the freed slaves. Viewed from the British perspective, most historical interest has focussed on the economic implications of the British switch from slaves to free labour. There are however other ways of assessing abolition.

Securing black freedom, if only, at first, in the Americas, was the culmination of a much longer process of British public debate about freedom. Taken together, the French Wars and the abolition movement had helped redefine British collective identity. The important work of Linda Colley has suggested the powerful sense of British cultural identity already in place at the accession of Victoria. Believing themselves to be empowered to export freedom, the British embarked on that creeping confrontation with other peoples, eager to secure their products, to gain access to their markets, and eager to impose on them the blessings of Christian freedoms – the very hallmarks of Britons themselves.

After 1838 the British were especially keen to assault slavery. Inevitably their imperial ventures brought them into contact with indigenous cultures which offended the British attachment to freedom. The British dilemma was how best to promote freedom while securing the greatest material and strategic advantages to themselves. Whatever the local outcome, and it varied enormously around the world, and however varied the tactical British response, they never lost sight of their ideological attachment to freedom.

It is easy in retrospect to see how this enterprise was doomed to failure. Yet it speaks to British self-confidence that they could even *contemplate* so awesome a task. This too was part of the formula. British cultural identity by the mid-nineteenth century hinged on a national self-confidence born of some dramatic political and military successes in the years 1789-1838. But it went much deeper than that. An urbanizing, literate people, linked by a web of political and religious institutions, and instructed through a plethora of printed materials, absorbed the language and the ideals of freedom. This was not simply a case of a political or religious elite cleverly orchestrating a public debate. For good or ill the British, of all sorts and conditions, had become wedded to the idea that they were, above all others, a freedom-loving people with an obligation to export their freedoms. The core of that belief was conceived in the initial objections to slavery, and honed and tuned in the campaign against slavery in the years 1787-1838.

Part III

THE AFRICAN DIASPORA

8 Black writers in their time

In recent times the study of Atlantic slavery has shifted from the edges of scholarly concerns to a central position in the study of Atlantic history. Indeed the concept of Atlantic history itself has been recast by the growing awareness of the importance of slavery. To a degree, this transformation in slave studies has reflected – and in its turn influenced – wider changes in patterns of historiography; the changing study of demography, of epidemiology, of food studies, of women's history, of social and, more recently, cultural history have all individually and collectively changed the very nature of academic history. In addition the subject has felt itself besieged in recent years by intellectual pressures from other disciplines which seemed, at times, to gnaw at the very fabric and respectability of history itself. No area of historical studies could hope to remain immune from these waves of intellectual challenge. Indeed our understanding of Atlantic slavery has been enriched by these wider historical changes (and sometimes passing fads). Looking back to the nature (and depth) of scholarship on slavery in the early 1960s is to be reminded not merely how much more we know about the subject, but how richer, more complex (and problematic) slave history has become – along with the study of history itself.

This is not to claim however that these changes in slave history merely confirm the idea of inevitable academic progress, or that contemporary scholarship stands as a reminder of earlier historians' shortcomings. On the contrary, it is important to remind ourselves of what we owe to earlier scholars whose work (even if now discarded or seriously challenged) provided the grounding of our current interests, and without which we could scarcely have begun our own work.

Occasionally however new themes have emerged which seem to have no obvious or clear-cut origins or roots in an earlier historiography; historical interests which appear to have sprung from thin air. This is strikingly so in the case of the black writers living in Britain in the late eighteenth century. In the great bulk of literature devoted to slavery, and to the story of abolition in Britain in the late eighteenth century, little attention was initially paid to the black writers whose lives and work now seem so important. Indeed those writers were often unknown to many historians working in the field. Yet today failure to mention black literature would be regarded as a major omission in any study of the mature Atlantic slave system or of abolition. We need then to ask ourselves: what has changed? What has pitched those writers to the forefront of attention when, a mere thirty years ago, they were unknown or ignored?

The most important force which served to bring black writers to recent scholarly attention was the pioneering work of historians and literary scholars of Africa. In both cases, black literature emerged not so much because of its intrinsic value or qualities but because of the changing social and political climate of the 1960s. Scholars – and later students in their thousands – rediscovered black literature as a direct consequence of the transformed cultural climate in the 1960s. The changing fortunes of the autobiography of Olaudah Equiano provide an entrée to these changes. Today Equiano is perhaps the best-known black writer from the era of British colonial slavery.[1] At any number of U. S. campus bookshops, stacks of the paperback version of his *Narrative* greet the new academic year. Unfortunately, they are not always the best, most serious, scholarly version – Carretta's Penguin edition, ¿There are countless courses which incorporate Equiano's writing either as a central text or as an important element in History and English courses. It is a book which sells in its thousands, and though the *Narrative* was a minor best-seller in its early years of 1789-1794 (thanks in the main to the author's indefatigable promotion of his own book), today's sales – and the present-day iconic status of the author – would surely have amazed (and delighted) the commercially minded Equiano.

This book's academic and commercial popularity needs some explanation. Thirty years ago few people had heard of Equiano, his book was scarce, and the academic courses he now dominates did not exist. Something fundamental has changed in the interval. Between 1789, when Equiano published his book, and his death in 1797 the author devoted his life to promoting and selling his *Narrative* throughout Britain. His promotions began on the tide of the early abolition campaign, and was carried forward on the initial enthusiasm for anti-slavery and, after 1791, for popular parliamentary reform. That initial surge of popular radicalism – of which Equiano was a part – was soon thoroughly staunched by the repressive loyalism of 1794 and later. Radical demands – for parliamentary reform or for ending the slave trade – had been transmuted, by the shadow of a violent and aggressive revolutionary France into subversive British Jacobinism. After 1794, and the arrests and trials of leading radicals (the leader – Thomas Hardy – was a friend of Equiano), radical agitation was driven into a frightened silence, its underground tradition kept alive by the wilder fringes of (mainly Irish) resistance. The mid-and late-1790s were cruel years for people of a reforming bent.

Equiano however continued with his book promotion, though operating quietly via friends and contacts, selling his intellectual wares in a private capacity, unconnected to any broader reforming group. He seems to have been a successful salesman, despite the generally intimidating political and social climate. When he married (in 1792) Equiano was described in the press – and in the provincial press at that – as 'well-known'.[2] When he died five years later, *The Gentleman's Magazine* listed his death in their 'Obituary of remarkable Persons.[3] Yet a few years after his death, Equiano was almost completely forgotten. A mere decade later, he was totally unknown to a publisher who re-issued the *Narrative*.[4] He had simply disappeared from view. Even when he was periodically republished (often in edited form) by Quakers, abolitionists or campaigners against American slavery in the 1830s to 1850s, the *real* Equiano remained unknown. His book had become useful as a literary quarry for those anxious to mine extracts for compilations devoted to accomplished 'people of colour', in the hope of illustrating the possibilities of black freedom. Equiano – or rather extracts from his book – had become a literary extra, a walk-on part in a grander political drama which seemed far removed from his own life and times.[5] True, his book was sometimes offered a niche in the roll-call of black attainments in the mid-century, but that simply took the form of a few pages culled from the *Narrative* and spliced into works by and about other Africans or their descendants. The whole was then offered to a reading public as literary proof of what blacks could achieve once the shackles of slavery were removed.[6] But this was very far removed from those remarkable days of the 1790s when Equiano criss-crossed Britain promoting his book, friend and acquaintance of the good and the great, and clearly revelling in his status as the most famous African in Britain. From the end of the American Civil War, Equiano disappeared utterly from view for a century.

Equiano was resurrected in 1960 by a prominent pioneer of African independence, the English Quaker Thomas Hodgkin. A passionate anti-colonial crusader, true to his Quaker roots, Hodgkin had a special interest in West Africa, particularly Nigeria. In 1960 (the year of Nigerian Independence from British rule) Hodgkin published his book *Nigerian Perspectives* – an anthology of Nigerian history. It was a path-breaking study of the nature and origins of that new African state, and included a major extract from Equiano's *Narrative*. Here then was Equiano revived as an African spokesman, an intellectual and literary forbear of West African nationalism. For those modern scholars who see Equiano as a prototype African-American writer – effectively the pioneer of the slave narrative – it is worth recalling that his modern reincarnation was in the form of an African, specifically a West African nationalist whose work was thought appropriate in the task of staking out a national identity.

In those same years, the early 1960s, another scholar, Paul Edwards was teaching at Fourah Bay College when he alighted on Equiano. Edwards's African students – previously fed a diet of almost uniquely English literary texts – demanded literature which seemed more appropriate to their needs and interests. Again, Equiano seemed to fit the bill. From that West African teaching experience Edwards embarked on his first re-publication of Equiano, in the process establishing his name as the pioneering scholar of Equiano and the man to whom subsequent scholars owe so much. In 1967 Edwards published *Equiano's Travels* in Heinemann's 'African Writers Series'. Quite independently, in that same year Philip Curtin, the eminent American historian of Africa, published *Africa Remembered,* an anthology which included a major extract from, and commentary on, Equiano.[7] Curtin was keen to direct students' attention towards African source materials and to alert American readers to the African background of African-Americans.

It seems a remarkable coincidence. Within the space of a mere seven years, three separate and unconnected scholars, each with very different interests and aims, had alighted on Equiano, whose writings had been invisible for a century past. Why, if he had remained forgotten for the past century, did his virtues and importance become so widely apparent in the early 1960s?

Of course Equiano is only the most famous of a number of black writers whose recent publishing careers have followed a similar if less spectacular path.

Gronniosaw, Phillis Wheatley, Francis Williams, John Marrant, Cugoano and – above all – Ignatius Sancho, were all published in Britain *before* Equiano. But all had been effectively ignored until their modern revival in the past thirty years.[8] The silence which fell on Equiano is perhaps surprising in the light of the fame and prominence he enjoyed in his own lifetime; the work of most other black writers was less substantial, simpler or less significant in other ways. Even so their works all share a similar story of decline and recent resurrection.

The most spectacular re-emergence has been enjoyed by Ignatius Sancho. In 1997 a major exhibition was held at the National Portrait Gallery in London to celebrate the life and times of Ignatius Sancho. Yet who, when Paul Edwards first re-issued Sancho's letters in 1968 (themselves published posthumously in 1782), knew about Sancho? Sancho's *Letters,* like Equiano's *Narrative,* went into several editions, the fifth and final version edited by his son in 1803. But thereafter – the silence of the grave. Sancho however had the advantage of having been painted by Thomas Gainsborough (who took a mere hour and forty minutes over the task) and his personal image has consequently remained in the public eye. The portrait, owned by the national Gallery of Canada in Ottawa, formed the centrepiece of the London exhibition and visitors were wooed towards the various artefacts on display by background music of Sancho's own composition. Clearly, Sancho left a more varied legacy of cultural attainments than did Equiano; a portrait by a major contemporary artist, music of an interesting quality and a series of letters – 159 in all – addressed to the good and the great. Sancho's reputation as a man of refinement and sensibility was well-founded. But to repeat the point, who knew about all this before 1968?[9]

Sancho and Equiano stand out from other eighteenth-century black writers for a number of obvious reasons. Their work was more substantial (in Sancho's case, more varied), and they occupied public positions which were denied other black contemporaries. Their recent prominence has been consequently more significant. Yet the same question – why the silence for more than a century? – applies with even greater force to the other black writers of the late eighteenth century. The most notable of those writers, Ottobah Cugoano, friend of Equiano and, like him, an activist against the slave trade, was in the public eye in the late 1780s and early 1790s. But he too vanished without trace until his major work, *Thoughts and Sentiments*, was re-issued, again by Paul Edwards, in 1969.

It is important to stress that we are discussing the British case; in North America, where slavery thrived in the nineteenth century, the situation was hugely different. In Britain we need to concentrate on two different contexts; the late eighteenth century – when black writers published their work and found a receptive audience – and the 1960s, when those same authors were revived (and to a degree re-invented). The initial contemporary interest in black writers appears to have been a direct consequence of the growing contemporary interest in slavery and the slave trade. Even the work of an earlier writer, Gronniosaw, may have been related to the public awareness of black issues in 1772 (the year of the Somerset Case).[10] But the three major figures whose work has dominated academic attention – Sancho, Cugoano and Equiano – were all published in the 1780s. What were the circumstances of that decade which sponsored this apparent flurry of black writing?

The first and most important fact was the existence of a British black community in the late eighteenth century. Even after thirty years of detailed research the precise size of that community remains uncertain. Though the earlier estimates from the 1970s now seem inflated, recent work has tended to be excessively conservative.[11] Whatever the demographic reality however, there is no doubting the mounting awareness in political and propertied circles, that London's black population had grown, and that it posed problems which troubled white contemporaries. It was a community augmented after 1783 by the return of British troops, loyalists and others from the British defeat in North America. Large numbers of slaves and ex-slaves had joined the British side in the conflict, often lured by the promise of freedom. Indeed the idea of arming slaves in that conflict was a potent threat which alarmed many – and not just the slave owners. The idea of an armed and aggressive body of freed slaves was the stuff of plantocratic nightmares (soon to be realized in St Domingue). In fact both sides tried to bolster their military fortunes by using black troops. And both sides treated those black troops more harshly than they did white troops. The defeated British faced a particular problem: what to do with the estimated 14,000 blacks who remained on their side when peace was signed?

Thousands were moved to Canada, and hundreds went to London. Some of them had been free men, property-owners for whom (along with white loyalists) the American defeat had meant ruin. Altogether, by 1786, there were more than 1,100 blacks from America in London, most of them in penury and dependent on charity. Their plight inevitably caught the eye; knots of black beggars seemed inescapable in London, and served to sharpen propertied concerns about the rise of urban (especially metropolitan) poverty. This interest in the 'black poor' became yet another element in the growing contemporary interest in black life in general.

As we have seen, there had been a black community – of sorts – for years past, with knots of Africans and their descendants living in the capital, or in the company of owners/employers across the face of Britain. But as long as that black presence was disparate and apparently usefully employed in the various tasks of domestic service, it raised no fundamental problems (except of course the persistent and nagging difficulty of the issue of whether slavery was legal in Britain).[12] It was *poverty* which focussed attention on local black life as never before.

Philanthropy had been the traditional solution to poverty, though in times of extreme sufferings national and local government had to flex their (rather puny) muscles to address the problem. Even then they tended, inevitably, to resort to the good will and charity of the propertied orders to contain distress. What happened in the 1780s however was quite different. Here was a colonial issue, black life (with overtones of slavery), thrust directly under the nose of London's well-to-do. The question was: what to do about it?

In the event the British opted for voluntary black migration. After the initial efforts at charitable relief were simply overwhelmed by the demands of the black poor, the government alighted on a scheme to 'repatriate' the blacks to Sierra Leone (though they also considered other sites). Later, a similar scheme was adopted for the black poor in Canada, whose privations were even worse, and clearly demanded attention. It seems, at one level, that the decision had been made that there was no place for blacks in Britain – or at least in London. In shipping them (admittedly with their co-operation) to West Africa, the British might appear to have decided to be without a domestic black community. We need to remind ourselves however that the Sierra Leone scheme was anchored at one point alongside another, more famous fleet, bound for an even more distant point of re-settlement: the 'First Fleet' of convicts bound for Botany Bay. And even that fleet had blacks among its numbers. Britain's determination was to deal with problem people by emigration, enforced or voluntary, ridding itself of domestic social difficulties by transporting those problems beyond the seas. In the late 1780s the main objects of these early schemes were the black poor and criminals. A precedent had been set and, a few years later, they were joined by clutches of radical dissenters whose activities proved difficult to contain in the revolutionary decade of the 1790s. In a different setting – but inspired by the same mentality – the British dealt with their rebellious slaves in the West Indies by shipping large numbers to the even more inhospitable environment of the Mosquito Coast. The last two decades of the eighteenth century saw, then, the British embark on some major movements of population: blacks from the capital and Canada to Africa, criminals and radicals to Australia, slaves from the West Indies to central America. It is within this context that we need to consider what happened to the black poor. And the question of the black poor – and of London's black population in general – forms the context for a discussion about the black writers in those same years.

Equiano came to public prominence in the unhappy events surrounding the Sierra Leone scheme. His friend Cugoano made himself known to the public in the same period. Both men capitalized on the notoriety of the Sierra Leone scheme – and the troubles which lay behind the scheme – to thrust themselves forward on the reading public. In fact both men were already known to prominent and influential people in London through their efforts to help fellow blacks (particularly in the recurring troubles of enslavement and transportation from London). Equiano was a friend of Granville Sharp and had long before brought black injustices and grievances to Sharp's attention. He had also been welcomed in other influential metropolitan circles in his efforts to find a spiritual home; to find a Christian church which satisfied him. Equiano was known to prominent clerics and politicians, and was familiar with Quakers – both in London and Philadelphia. Indeed the government's decision to choose Equiano as an agent for the Sierra Leone scheme only makes sense when we remember that he had already established his name as an intelligent, literate numerate and reliable man. Equiano had emerged as *the* African in London; the man to consult and to use in any dealings which officialdom might have with other blacks in the city.

For his part, Cugoano – altogether less prominent and well-known than Equiano – seems to have made himself known to public figures from 1786 onwards, again with an eye to seeking patronage or to help in the agitation against the slave trade.[13] A year later he published his tract *Thoughts and Sentiments*. It was a publication which Equiano seemed to have a hand in and there is internal evidence, as Carretta points out, which suggests that Cugoano saw the campaign against the slave trade as 'a kind of group project.' It is equally clear that Cugoano's work was influenced by other contemporary publications and arguments against the slave trade, notably Thomas Clarkson's earlier pioneering writing.[14] Along with Equiano and other Africans working in London, Cugoano published a number of letters in the London press in the years 1787-1789 on issues ranging from Sierra Leone to the campaign against the slave trade. No one at the time (or during the past thirty years) suggested that Cugoano was as significant a figure as his friend Equiano. Yet both men were, in the short term at least, clearly men of their times, brought to public attention by that particular chemistry of events in London in the 1780s. Clearly this is not to suggest they were not instrumental in securing their own fame or prominence; it is impossible to study Equiano without being struck by his drive and determination to establish a name for himself and, if possible, to make money *en route*. It was however the context which enabled both men to thrive. And that context was the distinctive – unique even – mix of black social-political experience in London in the mid-1780s.

That group of miserable blacks – the black poor (the generic term itself has become a label for the black presence) – which became so obvious in the 1780s came to represent the broader issue of Britain's massive slave empire. It had been relatively easy for West Indian planters and their scribes to keep critics of their system at arm's length over the previous century or so. Slavery was after all a distant institution. It thrived a long way away from Britain, on the high seas, in Africa and in the Americas. Britain seemed at one level only marginally involved, a mere bystander in the unfolding of major changes thousands of miles away. Of course we know that this accident of distance – another variant on the tyranny of distance – was utterly deceptive and that Britain, as this book has been at pains to suggest, was central to the whole process. Viewed from Britain however it is easy to imagine that slavery seemed merely noises offstage, the unfolding of distant colonial issues. Here the black community in London by the mid-1780s was critical, for it served to bring those broader issues centre stage, and to place them at the heart of metropolitan discussion. When looking into the faces of the mendicant blacks in London in the late eighteenth century, it was impossible to persist in the feeling that slavery was simply a distant, foreign concern. The enslaved chickens had come home to roost. Moreover one feature of the work of the black writers in the 1780s was their determination to ensure that the British were reminded of this fact and that they would *not* forget the plight of blacks throughout the Atlantic slave empire. In the words of a brief but telling aside by Equiano (in a letter to a clerical friend), 'Pray mind the Africans from the Pulpits.'[15]

From 1786 onwards, in the public dealings, the Africans in London – led by Equiano – impressed themselves on their readers and their political targets as spokesmen and representatives of Africans everywhere. The very concept of *being*

African was alien to Africans in the eighteenth century; their identity was shaped by their specific cultural-ethnic group, most notably (in terms of where most British slaves came from in the eighteenth century) their Igbo origins. It was outsiders, including the British, who saw and described Africans as 'Africans'. But this began to change in the late eighteenth century when Equiano and others around him began to adopt the terms 'Africans', 'Ethiopians', 'Sons of Africans' to describe themselves in letters to the press, and in dealings with friends and supporters. Both Cugoano and Equiano described themselves as 'African' on the title pages of their books. They were, then, speaking not simply as individual Africans but as voices for a broader community which stretched from London to the slave barracoons of West Africa and to the plantations of the Americas. More immediately of course they spoke for London's black poor, cast adrift, the flotsam and jetsam of Britain's changing Atlantic fortunes.

The British debate about slavery – about its morality and utility – was obviously not initiated by these African writers, who were, in some respects, merely bringing the voice of African experience to a debate which had already begun to influence British political life. It is also clear that earlier publications about the slave trade (notably by Clarkson) had influenced both Equiano and Cugoano in their own work. But what needs to be recognized is that both men helped to turn the growing concerns about special parochial matters (the black poor) into a broader discussion about slavery in its wider setting. Both men had established their name – among sympathizers and then to a large readership – through published political concerns for local people and issues: for blacks faced with either enslavement and/or transportation from England, and for the varied and complex difficulties facing the black poor in London. They are remembered however for an altogether grander achievement: in brief, for pioneering black writing.

It is striking however that the one man more responsible than any other for launching the public face of abolition, for gathering the data and ensuring that abolition had a firm argument to advance – Thomas Clarkson – paid no heed to blacks in Britain, nor to black writers. In 1808 when Clarkson published his own account of the events which led to the abolition of the slave trade in 1807 he listed, in chronological order, the sequence of books and publications which shaped abolition sentiment from the mid century onwards. He did not mention Equiano – and did not discuss the role or importance (if any) of the problems of the black poor in the 1780s.[16] It was in effect the beginning of a very long period of silence which descended on black writers – indeed, on black British history. Equiano, as we have seen, was periodically resurrected in extract form to be used in this or that changing campaign against slavery in North America. There were of course other black voices – African-Americans – whose names and books have remained far better known than Equiano's.

Times had changed and the issues that British black writers addressed had themselves changed. British colonial slavery was ended in 1838. And the British, having been instrumental in ending both the slave trade and slavery, were transmuted into that remarkably effective (and pious) anti-slavery nation of the nineteenth century. Anti-slavery thereafter became a pronounced feature of British life and of British overseas dealings. It was a stunning role-reversal (which the British themselves seemed not to notive): the greatest of eighteenth-century slave traders had reinvented themselves as the world's greatest abolitionist nation. In the process, the old literatures, the old arguments from the abolitionist debates of the late eighteenth century, seemed merely period pieces – dated curiosities of little relevance to the world of the mid- and late nineteenth century. Put simply, it was hard to see the relevance or utility of eighteenth-century black British writers. North America had its own black writers to call on, while the issues that had shaped those earlier British writers, and which they addressed in the 1780s, were only dimly remembered and were at best of only marginal utility in the campaigns against (especially) North American slavery.

If Equiano and friends were forgotten so quickly and so thoroughly, their publications unremembered, their names unknown, even the very community from which they sprang overlooked, how did modern scholars rediscover them – and why have those writers taken on so remarkable a modern status. ? For that, again, we need to recall the context.

Equiano was rediscovered *as an African.* In a period of emergent self-awareness among colonial peoples, Equiano's voice had immense appeal. It was an appeal which rapidly spread to North America – and even to Britain (on the back of a changing British black community from the 1960s onwards). In the drive for black freedom – broadly defined – earlier black voices were both useful and important. They were at once arresting and potentially useful in the struggle to shape a new black identity. Equiano's first reincarnation was in a paperback series aimed at an African readership. There is no need here to retrace the story of colonial independence from Britain, but in the aftermath of World War II (a war with its own seismic ideological concepts of freedom and self determination) the genie of political freedom escaped from the colonial bottle. In retrospect it is remarkable how quickly colonial freedom came to the peoples of the old British Empire, despite a stiff British rearguard resistance. The British lowered their flags and retreated to their distant islands. Political independence was not enough however. There was a need for an intellectual and educational re-thinking and restructuring of local life – a cutting loose from that strictly British cultural diet which had been the basis of so much colonial life and governance. New schooling, university systems needed to pay attention to *local* rather than metropolitan needs. New generations of teachers and writers sought to address local concerns; to define a history, literature and general intellectual legacy which was not simply derived from, or dictated by, former colonial governors. This was especially notable in the new universities.

In Africa and the West Indies, the educational diet began to change. A younger generation of scholars – especially in Africa and the West Indies – rebelled against an ethnocentric culture, seeking instead a more balanced, relevant and acceptable educational culture. It was easy, now, to see the attractions of Equiano.

But the attractions of Equiano (and here I use him to personify a broader cultural change) went far beyond former colonies. Today for example there is an

Equiano Society in London, founded to honour Equiano's memory and to promote 'the education of the public about the life and work of Olaudah Equiano... [and to] promote the education of the public about the contribution of African and Caribbean people who have made outstanding contributions to the Arts, Culture, and to the well-being of Britain during the past 400 years.' This simple assertion is based on an awareness of and an engagement with British black history which, a mere thirty years ago, was simply not possible. In the mid-1960s there had been no serious study of the history of the British black community – just as Equiano's own work was virtually unknown. Of course, the British black community of the mid-1960s was itself of recent vintage – and was reeling from the recently introduced restrictions on immigration into Britain. By and large, it was a community shaped by immigration since 1945, and few people made the important link between those post-1945 migrations and the earlier black communities of the seventeenth and eighteenth centuries. Again – and paralleling the revival of Equiano – the early reconstruction of the continuity of British black history only effectively began in the 1960s.[17] Thereafter there was a flurry of scholarly and popular explorations which provided the data, and offered a structure, for locating black society in its defining historical context. It is within that context that Equiano clearly had a role and a voice. Today, in the UK, Equiano has taken on an iconic status, the subject of exhibitions, films, biographies, radio programmes – and a place in the Millennium Dome.

A parallel story unfolded in the USA, where the transformations in Afrcian-American life after the 1960s were enormous. Moreover, the incorporation of African and African-American history into the mainstream American educational regime has been even more striking. Once again, Equiano's *Narrative* has been co-opted to the task. Equiano at his entrepreneurial best would surely have admired the way his book now sells, in numbers he could scarcely have dreamt of. Yet in the USA, as in the UK and West Africa, Equiano's role – his voice – can only be explained in terms of the fundamental upheavals in social and cultural life over the last thirty years. A similar explanation can be applied for the other black writers of the eighteenth and nineteenth centuries. They were people who wrote for – who were defined by – their particular time. And yet their real value and significance has only been revealed two centuries later, in the post-colonial world of the late twentieth century. The fact that their words continue to have a resonance, two centuries after their death, attests to the significance of the issue they addressed: the black diaspora, of which the writers formed a small but unusually influential part.

9 Who was the real Olaudah Equiano?

We remember Olaudah Equiano as a former slave who, despite all the sufferings that Atlantic slavery could heap on him, managed to create a decent life for himself. Of course, he was only one among millions; a single voice whose very unusualness catches the eye. How many other former slaves were so successful? How many others are even remembered? Yet it is the very distinctiveness of Equiano – especially his writing – which enables us to tease from his life a story of broader significance. Both then, and today, Equiano spoke for others whose voices went unrecorded.

Equiano was born into an Igbo family in what is now eastern Nigeria about 1745. He came from a prosperous home; his father was a local elder. Equiano's account of his African background, remembered and described more than forty years later, provides us with one of the few first hand African accounts of the details of contemporary African life, as it was lived far from the European gaze. In the mid-eighteenth century Europeans clung precariously to the African coastline, and knew little of the interior, save what they gleaned from the millions of Africans who poured through the slave barracoons *en route* to the Americas. Seized at the age of ten or eleven, Equiano was hauled to the coast by a series of African slave traders, travelling for months down complex routes before finally meeting the Europeans and their sailing ships, riding at anchor and awaiting their human cargoes for shipment to the Americas.

Equiano's account of enslavement to the white man, the grotesqueness of life on the infernal Atlantic crossing, and the terrors of re-sale in the Americas, has captured the historical imagination. Time and again, Equiano's account has been told and retold, anthologized and repeated by dozens of scholars and broadcasters on both sides of the Atlantic. Despite the wealth of data produced by demographic historians, this stark account by a single African survivor remains perhaps the most vivid and best-remembered image of black Atlantic slavery.

After a short stay in Barbados, (the favourite first landfall for many British ships – thanks to its easterly location), Equiano was transported, on another ship, to Virginia. At the time Virginia was the heart of the Chesapeake tobacco industry, its slave-grown tobacco cultivated on hundreds of plantations which fringed the edges of that massive water-system. Each year, the crop was shipped in growing volume across the Atlantic; eighteenth-century Glasgow thrived on the business of handling, packing and selling-on the tons of slave-grown tobacco. But Equiano was not destined for work in tobacco. Instead – and like many other Africans – he was employed as a slave sailor. The British merchant marine and the Royal Navy regularly used Africans, and their New-World descendants, as crew and as stewards. And it was on British ships that the enslaved Equiano learned the skills and developed the talents which served him in such good stead in later life.

He was, first of all, renamed. Africans were commonly given new names by their British owners. Planters, sailors, propertied Britons, all tended to prefer their own choice of names for the Africans they employed. Equiano was, variously, renamed Jacob, Michael, Daniel and – most lasting of all Gustavus Vassa. Later, though Equiano used this, his African name, in his public and published persona, in private (in handwritten letters and to his friends) he seems to have preferred to be known as Gustavus Vassa. Behind this confusion of names lay a central fact of slave life; that here were people, uprooted from their past and given new identities by whites who wished to refashion them in a different (i.e. a non-African) image. But what names *did* Africans use among themselves; what did they call each other? Did they cling to their African identity – as they clung to other features of their African cultures? Though we know Equiano by his African name, he seems to have called himself Gustavus Vassa , adding the term, 'the African' late in life.

Along with his new names, Equiano acquired a new religion. Converted – again on board a British ship – Equiano became ever-more devout, ending his life as a staunch Methodist. At the same time, Equiano acquired the rudiments of literacy – and even basic arithmetic (which proved so important in his later business life) – and all from other British sailors. By the time he made his first visit to England in 1757, as a 12 year African slave/sailor, Equiano showed all the qualities which were to flourish in his adult life. Two years later, in February 1759 he was formally baptized in St Margaret's Westminster – taking the name Gustavus Vassa.

Equiano was not a typical slave (one working in the sugar or tobacco fields), for his working life was fashioned at sea. These were the years of expansive British maritime and commercial power, regularly locked in a struggle for global pre-eminence with the French. On Royal Navy ships in the 1760s and 1770s, Equiano saw action in the Mediterranean, the Channel and North America. He even served on the British expedition to the Arctic in 1772. Again, he was unusual in the range of his experiences, but we need to remind ourselves that untold legions of Africans were scattered to the far edges of British trade and dominion by the rapacious forces of Atlantic slavery. Though the very great majority of all African slaves were destined for the Americas (and the majority of those destined for the sugar fields), others found themselves, like Equiano, cast around the edges of the Atlantic world – as fashionable black servants throughout Western Europe, as sailors on vessels plying their trade world-wide – as refugees in the frozen settlements of Canada; even, as criminals, in the early penal settlements of Australia. This was a diaspora which took the faces and voices of Africa clean round the world by the late eighteenth century. But of all those faces, Equiano's remains perhaps the best-known.

On board various British ships, Equiano began to reveal a host of qualities; hard work, budding entrepreneurial skills (money saved on ship from a variety of tasks) emergent independence and ambition. But he was still a slave. Promised his freedom – or so he thought – Equiano found himself sold yet again, in 1762 from one ship to another in the Thames. Whatever English law said about the legality and status of slavery in England (and it was a confusing message), the social reality was clear enough; blacks continued to be sold – though admittedly in small numbers. For a start, slaves remained more valuable in the Americas. But returning planters, colonial and military officials, and sailors, employed blacks as slaves – and occasionally sold them on. Such was Equiano's fate. Thinking himself free on board a ship in England, he found himself sold back to the Caribbean – still a sailor – but still a slave.

Based in Montserrat in the 1760s, Equiano worked up and down the Caribbean, and between the islands and the major seaports of North America. Always alert to commercial opportunities, he supplemented his earnings by trading. He bought glassware in one island, sold it at a profit elsewhere; he took citrus, sugar and, barrels of pork from one place to another; he sold turkeys from South Carolina to Montserrat and 'gained near three hundred percent on them'. His captain jibbed at Equiano's request to transport cattle between the islands. But wherever he sailed, Equiano looked for commercial sidelines, 'ever trading as I went.' Yet this man was still a slave; keeping his cash in a chest on board the ship, alert to the regular threats and scams whites invariably tried on slaves (refusing to pay, threatening them with violence). Money figured large in his life; he worked hard to make it, he kept careful records of profit and loss – and he talked about it a great deal (though we need to remember that he was keen to cultivate a favourable impression among his British readers.)

By 1766 Equiano had saved enough to buy his freedom. He had raised the question of freedom a number of times with his owner (a Quaker trader in Montserrat). Finally, in 1766, he accepted £70 cash (in local money) from Equiano in return for a certificate of manumission. Freedom alone was not enough, though; Equiano could not wait to quit the West Indies and his heart was 'fixed on London…'. Whatever the continuing dangers and disadvantages, London seemed infinitely preferable to the horrors of life in the slave societies of the West Indies.

How did a slave manage to earn and save money on this scale? How could people, wrenched from their African homelands, who stumbled ashore in the New World with virtually nothing, make such improvements in their material lives? We are so accustomed to thinking of slavery as a mean, vicious system, that it seems hard to understand Equiano's rising material well-being. In fact, he was in good company; there were many slaves who secured for themselves a more decent material life than we might expect. By 1800 for example we know that something like 20% of all the spare cash in Jamaica was in slave hands. Slave crimes included slaves stealing items from each other; stealing household fittings, clothing, pots – small luxuries even. Slaves sold animals, foodstuffs, items they had made, to their white owners and to neighbours. Planters' tables were loaded with foodstuffs bought from local markets – and those markets were worked by slaves, selling, buying and exchanging goods they had grown, cured or acquired in their spare time. Beneath the surface of the slave systems of the Americas, there were areas of independent slave activity which were exploited by slaves who were industrious, imaginative and enterprising, to create for themselves a better material life. Few did it to better effect than Equiano.

From 1767 onwards, Equiano's home base was England, but he continued to spend much of his time at sea. Each voyage, each mission, afforded new ways of earning cash; shaving his fellow shipmates, cutting their hair, buying goods here, selling them elsewhere at a profit. Always alert to profitable trade – and ever vigilant towards whites who were likely to cheat or threaten him. He was even employed to organize and ship African slaves (from one island to another) and in the management of a settlement on the Mosquito Coast . But being in charge of slaves was work which made him unhappy, though he was in no position to resist. Even as a free black, Equiano remained vulnerable, like so many others, to the inherent dangers and threats which formed the backcloth to black life throughout the African diaspora.

On shore Equiano drifted in and out of jobs in London, sometimes unemployed, but always keen to work. In his idle moments, he found himself increasingly troubled by his faith, wandering between churches and spiritual advisors, before finding his true spiritual home among the Methodists. He even contemplated life as a missionary. More worrying still perhaps, Equiano, like other blacks in England, was periodically threatened by re-enslavement. Time and again, slave captains and merchants threatened to seize blacks in London and ship them, against their wishes, to the Americas (where they could be used – or sold – more profitably than in England). After the infamous Somerset Case in 1772, the law decreed that blacks could not be removed from England against their wishes (under the terms of the Habeas Corpus Act). Yet this did not totally prevent such kidnappings happening. Poor blacks – especially those close to the water's edge – faced regular threats of transportation. It was a danger which would not cease until slavery in the British colonies was ended (and that not until 1834.)

In his search for a satisfactory spiritual home, Equiano had moved among London's Quakers. But he had also, by the early 1770s, made himself known to critical political figures in the capital. When faced by the practical problems and dangers confronting fellow blacks in London, Equiano turned in 1774 to Granville Sharp 'that well-known philanthropist'. It proved an important alliance, for Equiano, who was emerging as a key figure in the local black community, was to liaise with Sharp on major issues in the story of the British black community over the next twenty years.

None was more critical – or grotesque – than the infamous *Zong* case, which Equiano raised with Sharp in 1783. In March of that year Equiano called on Sharp to tell him that some 130 Africans had been drowned, thrown overboard from a Liverpool slave ship. Even by the standards of the day, the *Zong* affair was extraordinary. Capt. Luke Collingwood's Liverpool ship, carrying 470 Africans bound for Jamaica, was running short of water, and Collingwood decided to ditch a large number of weaker Africans in order to secure the survival of the rest – and then to claim the loss of the murdered slaves on the ship's insurance. Despite the initial objections from the crew, in the end 131 Africans were murdered in this way.

When the case surfaced in an English court it did so as a contested insurance issue – not as a murder case. Though the case petered out, the details shocked observers, even though they were accustomed to regular stories of cruelties and death on board British slave ships. Yet it is also instructive to know that the outrage brought together London's most prominent African, Equiano, and Sharp, the man who had established himself as the most active friend of blacks living in England. Here was a black-white alliance which proved important in the genesis of the early campaign against the slave trade itself.

The *Zong* case was exceptional in its scale. Yet it was only an extreme form of the violence basic to the Atlantic slaving system. Moreover it was a system which intimately involved the British. The 11,000 British slave voyages, the rise of Bristol, Liverpool and Glasgow (and a host of smaller ports), the links between the British hinterland economies and the Atlantic trade – all and more confirmed what Equiano and other African knew from bitter first hand experience; that British Atlantic prosperity thrived on African immiseration. What was needed was an attack on the slave trade itself.

As Equiano sailed on regular commercial voyages across the Atlantic, and from North America to the West Indies in the 1770s and early 1780s, he continued to make the most of every passing commercial opportunity. More important still though were the lessons he learned on his regular visits to Philadelphia, his ' favourite old town'. There he was deeply impressed by the work and the attitude of local Quakers, and was especially struck by their treatment of slaves and free blacks. Philadelphia Quakers had established a free school for Philadelphia blacks. These Philadelphia experiences clearly left their mark, and Equiano was to turn to London's powerful Quakers in his first efforts against the slave trade. It seemed natural enough that, in 1785, he should lead a deputation of London blacks to petition London Quakers to promote the interests of 'the poor, oppressed, needy, and much degraded negroes', thanking the Quakers for their efforts 'towards breaking the yoke of slavery'.

By the mid-1780s the British could scarcely avoid the domestic consequences of Atlantic slavery. British life had, in the course of the eighteenth century, been transformed by the fruits of slave labours and by the rise of sugar and tobacco consumption. But slavery flourished on the far side of the Atlantic, in the Americas. Africans and their descendants could be found scattered across the face of Britain, notably in the capital, in fashionable watering places and stately homes, serving the needs of their propertied owners/employers, and providing, through their exotic colour, a social cache for their owners. But it was the expanding black community in London in the 1780s which began to catch the eye – and caused growing domestic friction among people (and government) unhappy to see the development of a sizeable black community in the capital.

The numbers of blacks in London increased in the wake of the British defeat in North America in 1783. It was from these circumstances, as we have seen, that the

Sierra Leone scheme emerged. Against his better judgement, Equiano accepted the post of commissary for the expedition, in charge of securing provisions for the black settlers destined for Africa. From the first, Equiano faced a plan replete with problems, not least the blatant corruption of a minor official, who pocketed money instead of providing clothing. When Equiano raised the matter with government officials he was dismissed. Efforts were then made to damage Equiano's name in the press. The proof of his case – and confirmation of his general unease – lay in the miserable fate of those settlers who finally sailed for Sierra Leone. In April 1787, 350 sailed from Plymouth; four years later only 60 survived. It was a scheme bedevilled with weakness and failings. To Equiano, the problem was simple. Some of the whites in charge treated the blacks 'the same as they do in the West Indies.' Equiano was saved from a premature end by his honesty.

By early 1787 Equiano had become a public figure in London. He was well-known in government circles, he moved with ease among Quakers and among other men of sensibility and his name was bandied about in the press. He had come a long way from his days of childhood slavery. He was now the most prominent African in London – and he was clearly edging towards political activity. It was understandable that he would build on his recent prominence and his experience, to promote the African cause. Equiano's first move, along with a group of other Africans in London, was to petition the Queen, in March 1787, seeking her support on behalf of the 'millions of my African countrymen, who groan under the lash in the West Indies.' It was a shrewd move, designed to capitalize on his own recent fame at a time of heightened interest in the Atlantic slave trade. Equiano's old associates, the Quakers, had begun to campaign against the slave trade, promoting that first wave of anti-slave trade petitions which began to flood Parliament in remarkable numbers (and containing tens of thousands of signatures from across the nation).

In this, the initial attack on the slave trade, Equiano played a remarkable part – though it is one which historians have been reluctant to concede. For a start his was an unusual voice. Here was a literate, devout and industrious African, a former slave, who spoke and wrote with an authority which outsiders could not match. The most important contribution Equiano could make to the abolitionist cause was to tell his own story; to regale his British readers and audiences with the story of his own remarkable life. Thus, he set out to write his autobiography, in the hope that it would add weight to the abolitionist cause. But he clearly hoped (and he succeeded) in profiting from his efforts. Just as in his days as a young slave travelling down the islands, Equiano saw the chance to make profit. His writing brought him profits beyond anything he had previously earned.

Equiano had acquired his literacy as a young boy on board ship. He had, at the same time, developed an interest in arithmetic (he was for ever computing his profits and percentages on this deal and that). By 1789 he was clearly an educated, sophisticated man, and his writing abounds with references to a string of major literary works. Equiano was a bookish man, but he was anxious to promote his bookishness – to regale his British readers with his attainments. His was, after all, a remarkable personal success story, the story of the rise of a man from the most wretched of conditions to a respected position in contemporary British society. Yet Equiano offered his readers much more than a tale of industrious and god-fearing self-improvement. His life stood in sharp contrast to that ideology of the slave-owning lobby (slave traders and planters alike) who had, for a century and more portrayed Africans and their new-world descendants as incorrigibly lazy. Only the rigours and constraints of slavery could, they argued, be relied on to keep slaves at work.

Equiano set out to write an autobiography which would be his personal contribution to the anti-slave trade campaign, though his own personal activities went back to 1774. But now, in 1789, he needed a national platform. To publish the book Equiano built up a formidable list of subscribers (people who subsidized the book by guaranteeing to buy it. The list of those names – with the sprinkling of the good and the great, aristocrats, politicians, and the famous from across the nation – provides a clear indication both of Equiano's prominence and his ability to rally powerful people to his side. He also secured sales outlets for the book at London's best-known bookseller. Later, he travelled the length and breadth of Britain, promoting new editions of the book in major towns – again using local subscribers to guarantee his initial costs.

The book – *The Interesting Narrative of the Life of Olaudah Equiano or Gustavus Vassa the African written by Himself* – was published in two volumes in 1789. It is a book which, though concerned with one man's struggle up from slavery, can be read at a number of levels. It belongs to the tradition of working class autobiographies that become so common in the nineteenth century. It is also the diary of a soul; the story of one man's spiritual odyssey. More recently, scholars (especially in North America) have been keen to locate Equiano's book at the heart of the slave narrative; here is the voice of an African in a world which had traditionally denied a voice to those millions cast ashore in the slave colonies of the Americas. We need however to think of it as American in its broadest setting – certainly not *North* American – since it speaks to and for Africans scattered around the vast geography of the Americas. After all, at the time Equiano wrote, it was the *African*, not the European, who was the critical and seminal immigrant in key areas of the Americas.

However we now interpret this book, for his part Equiano had a simpler task in hand. He wanted to sell as many copies of his book as possible. To that end he published various editions of the book in his lifetime, spent months on the road promoting and selling copies, in a promotional sweep which would be familiar to modern publishers. Between 1789 and his death in 1797, Eqiuano supervised nine different editions. It was also published in Dutch, Russian, German, in New York as well as Dublin, Edinburgh and Norwich. It was, by the standards of the time, a best seller.

Equiano made changes to each successive edition, incorporating new arguments and facts, shifting the argument this way and that. Most crucially of all, he began to promote a much harder political line than other abolitionists. Sometimes he floated an idea in letters to the press, then incorporated those arguments in later editions of the book. Thus, in the last edition published in the year he died in 1797, he developed an new economic argument in favour of abolishing the slave trade. The planters in West Indian slave colonies, and the slave traders, could scarcely imagine life without the regular arrivals of African slaves. Equiano turned their argument around; imagine what material bounty and economic well-being would flow from a free trade to and from Africa. End the slave trade and Africa beckoned as a massive market for British goods, a source of untold raw materials and a commercial future of untold prosperity. His was a plea for free trade which, though already advanced by Adam Smith in 1776, had not been effectively marshalled against the Atlantic slave empire. Equiano saw a future which linked an expansive Britain to a prospering – but free – Africa. It was an argument which predicted an economic critique of slavery. Yet, in 1797, it was an distinctive plea – and it came from an African.

As he moved around the country in the 1790s, Equiano travelled on familiar terms with radicals and reformers, who provided a ready-made network both for his travels and for his book sales. It was a network however which was disrupted – and silenced – by that reactionary hostility to all reforming issues which was sponsored by the government, fearful of revolutionary France. Some of Equiano's friends were jailed, others were slandered as revolutionaries. But Equiano persevered, promoting the abolitionist cause through his autobiography. Even his marriage to Sarah Cullen, an English woman, in 1792 and the birth of their two daughters did not deflect him. His book brought domestic material security. But it did not last long, for Equiano died on March 31st 1797. His estate yielded almost £1,000 to his surviving descendants (perhaps £80,000 in today's terms). Though it was a large amount, it is scarcely surprising to those who know about Equiano's entrepreneurial past. After all, Equiano had been profiting, pennies at a time, since his early days as an enslaved youth.

Today, two hundred years on, where does Equiano belong? He has become an iconic figure, one of the best-remembered Africans of his age – an age which was dominated by the ramifications of the enslaved African diaspora. More people read Equiano today than in his lifetime. His words are quoted by those historians keen to capture the human reality of the African experience on the slave ships and in the Americas. Yet his was a single voice, speaking about one man's life. In truth, of course Equiano speaks, two hundred years on, for much more than one man's experience. As he himself was aware, he wrote and spoke for others, for those armies of fellow Africans uprooted from their homelands and hauled, through the trauma of the slave ships, to a lifetime's bondage in the Americas. When we think of Equiano, when we read his autobiography, it is worth remembering those millions whose voices went unheard but whose labours brought into being a world of such familiarity that we take it for granted. Our sweetened tastes, our tobacco, all and more flowed from the sweat of Africans and their descendants across the Americas. Whatever else Equiano might have achieved in his remarkable life, he left a literary monument to those forgotten millions.

10 Ignatius Sancho: an African man of letters

Ignatius Sancho was born a slave in 1729, to a slave mother (who died shortly afterwards) on board an Atlantic slave ship heading for the Americas. At the time of Sancho's birth, the British were fast becoming the most successful and most prosperous of European slave-traders. But the human cost of these European profits and the pleasure they brought, was a catastrophe visited upon large regions of Africa, and upon those Africans violently scattered around the edges of the British Atlantic slave system. There were millions, like Sancho's mother, who were plucked from African homelands to toil in the Americas.

Though in many respects the slaves' efforts, on the far side of the Atlantic, were not immediately obvious to Europeans, tending instead to be taken for granted, Sancho's life is a reminder that the slave experience was often more visible and direct than we might sometimes imagine. For a start, Sancho like many other slaves made his home in Britain. Given the vast numbers of Africans involved, it was inevitable that some, like Sancho, would find their way to Britain.

Sancho was brought to Britain as a small child, where he worked for three sisters in Greenwich, at a period when fashion decreed the use of black domestics, both enslaved and free. A black page or servant was commonplace in the homes of the wealthy, in London, in fashionable spas and in stately homes, a fact amply confirmed in any number of eighteenth-century portraits. Black servants were trained up in the domestic skills and social graces expected by their owners and were dressed often in elaborate (sometimes bizarre) attire, both to catch the eye and to impress visitors and friends. Like other blacks, Sancho took the opportunity to improve himself, with the help of friends and the support of those who had noticed his abilities and industry. The Duke of Montagu, who spotted him early, gave him books and Sancho quickly took to studying. But, to the horrified disapproval of his female owners, he also loved female company, and he ran away, at the age of 20, to seek refuge in the Montagu household. There, working as a butler, he flourished, reading voraciously, writing prose, poetry and music. He became an avid theatregoer, a fan of Garrick, and became a figure in fashionable London society; friendly with actors, painters and, most interestingly, with Laurence Sterne.[1]

By the late 1760s Sancho had made the transition from being a decorative black domestic to a man of refinement and accomplishment, penning letters to friends and sympathizers around the country. In 1773 he was able to quit the life of a domestic servant and set up as a shopkeeper in Westminster, thanks to a small bequest from the Duke of Montagu. With this modest backing, Sancho moved into a shop in Charles Street Westminster, with his black wife Anne and their expanding family, eventually of six children whom he affectionately called his 'Sanchonettas'. Such shops were relatively simple and cheap affairs. An investment of a mere £10 could yield an annual income of £50, and though London – especially Oxford St – quickly established a reputation for its dazzling array of extravagant shops, Sancho's was much more typical (they were often little more than a counter in a front room).

As Sancho tended to his counter and customers – taking tea with favoured or famous clients – his wife Anne worked in the background, breaking down the sugar loaves into the smaller parcels and packets required for everyday use. Slave-grown sugar, repackaged and sold by black residents of London, themselves descendants of slaves; here was a scene rich in the realities and the symbolism of Britain's slave-based empire. Among the prominent visitors to Sancho's shop was Charles James Fox, leader of contemporary parliamentary radicals. We know that Sancho voted for Fox at the 1780 election. This ex-slave had acquired the right to vote by his property rights as a shop keeper in Westminster. From what we know of Sancho's views, it is not surprising that he voted for Fox, but it is surely remarkable that at the high water-mark of British slavery a black should cast a vote in a British election.

In an increasingly commercialized and competitive world, Sancho, like other contemporary shopkeepers, promoted his wares as best he could; through advertisements in their windows, above their doors, and in local handbills and newspapers. Sancho also used a trade card, depicting his most important commercial item – tobacco. His card provides a telling picture, portraying all those elements of tobacco production which proved so exploitative for so many people. It contains images of an American Indian, and of black slaves gathering the tobacco. On closer inspection the image of slave work looks much more like slaves gathering sugar than tobacco, yet the precision of the image is not the key point. What matters is the message. Here was a product – tobacco – which was brought forth by slaves for the pleasure and profit of Europeans, and was sold by an ex-slave shop-keeper in London. Sancho's trade card is another reminder, if we need none, of the centrality of slavery to eighteenth-century British trade commerce and commerce.

Ignatius Sancho is better known as a correspondent than as a shopkeeper. He made himself known to men and women of sensibility throughout the country. He contacted Laurence Sterne for example, lodged in his remote Yorkshire vicarage, to praise his work and to bring to Sterne's attention the plight of enslaved Africans. In fact, Sterne had already taken up the issue. Moreover, the complexities of slavery had already surfaced in the series of slave cases in English courts and widely reported in newspapers. In the year Sancho was born, 1729, an important legal ruling had issued from the Attorney and Solicitor Generals following a petition from West India interests, concerned about their rights over slaves imported into England. The law officers decreed that

> ... a slave, by coming from the West Indies, either with or without his master, to Great Britain or Ireland, doth not become free... We are also of opinion, that the master may legally compel him to return to the plantations.

Twenty years later, the Lord Chancellor, Lord Hardwicke, (in 1749) re-affirmed this earlier Yorke-Talbot judgement; ruling that slavery *was* legally sanctioned in England. He ruled that the common belief that,

> the moment a slave sets foot in *England* he becomes free, has no weight with it, nor can any reason be found, why they should not be equally so when they set foot in *Jamaica,* or any other *English* plantation...

Yet legal judgement continued to be confused, and other judges made contrary rulings. Of course the legal fraternity was aware that any definitive freeing of slaves in Britain would form a breach in the previously secure British slave system. If slaves were to be freed in Britain, why not in the colonies? Those slave colonies however continued to be the hub of unquestioned British material well-being; remove slavery which underpinned those colonies, and British economic interests would be damaged.

In practice (as we have seen) slavery *did* exist in Britain, and could be seen in the number of slave sales and slave runaways announced in eighteenth-century newspapers. How could it have been otherwise, with such large-scale movements of people and ships between the African slave coast, the slave colonies of the Americas and Britain? It was only natural then, that Africans and American-born blacks began to appear throughout Britain. Sancho was one of many.

In the decade before his death in late 1780, Sancho, now in his forties, became an inveterate letter-writer. He had made earlier attempts at writing but his subsequent reputation was founded on the letters he penned in the 1770s. Was it mere accident that the very great majority of his letters were drafted when he had quit domestic service and had become a shopkeeper? Or did the life of a simple grocer allow Sancho the time and circumstances to dispatch letters to all and sundry, prompted no doubt by that world of political and polite gossip which passed through his shop. He was now party to a social world previously denied him as a domestic. The status of service had been left behind and Sancho was free to communicate directly with customers, and in his spare moments by letter to distant correspondents. The nature and style of his letters, suggest that Sancho had disciplined himself in a style he thought appropriate for the intended correspondents and there seems little doubt that his basic literary style was greatly influenced by Laurence Sterne.

Sancho's reputation as a letter-writer had first been established by the publication of Sterne's own letters in 1775. Sancho's initial contact with Sterne (in 1766) had been to praise *Tristram Shandy* in a letter which mixed praise with excessive sentimentality.

> Of all my favourite authors, not one has drawn a tear in favour of my miserable black brethren – excepting yourself and the human author of Sir George Ellison.

Sancho urged Sterne to speak out on behalf of 'the uplifted hands of thousands of my brother Moors.' Sterne's response to Sancho's elaborate approaches seems to have encouraged the subsequent wave of letters which Sancho dispatched right and left, once he had more time on his hands as a shopkeeper. These letters form a rare insight into the life and times of an ex-slave living in eighteenth England.

Sancho's writing provides much more than a glimpse of an interesting if distinctive late eighteenth-century figure. They take us to the very heart of the black experience at the height of the enslaved African diaspora. Time and again, Sancho speaks about – speaks for – his fellow Africans, and about slavery 'as it is at this time practiced in our West Indies.' But Sancho also spoke about the fate of the British black community, which was itself forged by slavery. The sole reason for the black presence in Britain was of course the Atlantic slave empire.

For much of the eighteenth century, as the material bounty yielded by slavery increased and diversified, any initial worries about the ethics of slavery were simply swamped. What would Glasgow have been without tobacco; how would Liverpool have fared without the slave trade? Economic self-interest simply overwhelmed whatever moral scruples contemporaries might have had about the enslavement of legions of Africans and about their immiseration on the far side of the Atlantic. It was a process which distance rendered more comfortable for the British. But the evolution of a black community in London, and the legal difficulties periodically thrown up by slave cases in English (and Scottish) courts, ensured that the broader problem of slavery became progressively more troublesome. Blacks in Britain, the slave cases in courts, the occasional black voice raised in anger – all and more ensured that the problem of slavery would not go away. It was this *domestic* British debate about slavery which formed the genesis of the early campaign against slavery. Though Quakers had been opposed to slavery since the late seventeenth century, they remained, despite their growing commercial power, a marginalized sect with little overt political influence. The first people in Britain to ponder and agitate effectively how best to undermine the Atlantic slave system became aware of the problem by events and individuals in Britain itself. It was the black British slave, the black British voice – the lot and the fate of blacks living in Britain – which made the first important dint in the previously untroubled defences of the West Indian slave system.

In this, Ignatius Sancho played an important role. Always ready to raise the question of slavery with his friends and acquaintances, his letters touched on the plight of Africans everywhere, and of the problems facing blacks in Britain. At times Sancho was open – even extravagant – in promoting the black cause. His letters to Sterne were perhaps the most blatant example of this mode of address, though he may have adopted Sterne's own mode of expression to make a point. (" Consider slavery – what it is – how bitter a draught – and how many have been made to drink of it!") More usual however was Sancho's passing references to the black experience; throw-away remarks about the occasional racial slur, the public insult and contemporary racist culture. Describing a family night out in London, he wrote;

> we went by water – had a coach home – were gazed at etc. etc. but
> *not much abused...* [my emphasis].

Why should Sancho make such a point, unless the contrary experience was commonplace? Why describe something which had *not* happened – except to show that the opposite was much more common? Sancho regularly reminded his correspondents about the abuse blacks were likely to receive in public. He reminded Soubise, another African servant (to the Duchess of Queensberry), of the 'ill-bred and heart-racking abuse of the foolish vulgar...'. At one point, despite a lifetime in England, Sancho described himself as, '...a lodger, and hardly that.'

At times he clearly despaired:

> to the English, from Othello to Sancho the big – we are either
> foolish – or mulish – all – all without a single exception.

Like his fellow blacks, Sancho could not avoid the periodic barbs of hostile, vulgar abuse, much of it directed at his colour. In private letters however he sometimes turned this on its head, revelling in his racial difference and wearing as a badge of pride what others used as an insult. In his late years, as he grew fatter, he described himself as 'a man of the convexity of belly exceeding Falstaff...' but adding 'and a black face into the bargain.' In another letter he spoke of being 'a coal-black, jolly African'. At other times he described himself as 'a poor Blacky grocer' and 'only a poor thick-lipped son of Afric...'. This jocularity in letters to his friends (to whom he sent 'Blackamoor greetings') never dimmed his sense of the wrongs done to unknown armies of his fellow Africans – 'my brother Negroes'. Nor did Sancho lose his sense of indignation of what Britain had done – and continued to do – to the peoples in Africa and other parts of the globe. And all for the pursuit of money.

> The grand object of English navigators – indeed of all Christian
> navigators – is money – money – money...

In pursuing this global commercial greed, the British had been 'uniformly wicked in the East – the West Indies – and even on the coast of Guinea.'

Understandably, Sancho was especially grieved about the fate of Africa and its slaves ('a subject that sours my blood') but he blamed African rulers as well as European traders for the evils visited upon the continent;

> ... the Christians' abominable Traffic for slave – and the horrid cruelty and treachery of the petty Kings...

From his first letter to Sterne in 1766 until his death fourteen years later, slavery hovered over Sancho's correspondence.

It was precisely in these same years that the question of slavery began its long complex gestation as a political and ethical issue in Britain, driven forward by a small band of indefatigable abolitionists and aided by the experiences of London's black community. After years of apparent indifference, anti-slavery was launched by the slave cases in English courts and by the attendant publicity and controversy. The campaign to secure black freedom in Britain, though fought initially on a narrowly defined front, had major implications for the slave empire. The West India lobby, long prominent in London as political and economic spokesmen and lobbyists for slave traders and planters, indeed for all involved in Atlantic slave trading, appreciated that their position was under threat. There thus began that political and publishing skirmishing – pitching friends of black freedom against supporters of the slave lobby – which was to continue, with varying degrees of intensity, for the next fifty years.

The intellectual roots of anti-slavery reached back further of course, more specifically to the writing of the French Enlightenment. But after 1789 abolition was transformed by the ideas of the French Revolution. The concept of the `Rights of Man' changed the wider debate about human and political rights (for black and white, for men and women) and was promoted by a vast flow of cheap publications, among them writings by black authors. Abolitionists pressed home the attack, arguing in Parliament that abolishing the Atlantic slave trade would bring the end of slavery in the Americas a little closer. In the short-term, progress was hindered by the violence of the French Revolution. But the abolition case was driven forward by massive public agitation, in print, in crowded local meetings and through a visual and material culture of anti-slavery; in pictures, prints, plaques, medallions and pottery. Some of that material left a permanent mark on the collective British memory, notably the plan of the Liverpool slave ship the *Brookes* and Wedgwood's medallion of the kneeling slave – `Am I not a man and a Brother?'

Throughout this campaign the slaves played a key part. Their voice was heard – and heeded – as never before. Black writers found their work adding to the groundswell of abolitionist sentiment. It was at this point that Ignatius

Sancho found a posthumous fame and influence. His letters had been collected and published two years after his death, in 1782. Over the next twenty years they were republished five times (ensuring an income from royalties to his widow, who continued to run his Westminster shop). It was a book which brought a tone of educated civility to the abolition debates. Here was an African – an ex-slave – confronting contemporaries on terms they recognized and admired. Literate, sophisticated (however stylized), Sancho provided evidence of black attainment and potential. In a world grown accustomed to thinking of the African as a beast of burden, suited only to the physical demands of colonial labour, Sancho's cultural and literary style caught the eye. Nor was he alone.

Abolitionists clearly appreciated the importance of employing black activists and writers in their campaign. Ottobah Cugoano, a London-based African, who added his personal experience to the abolition cause in a book first published in 1787, pushed the abolitionist case further than most. He demanded total black freedom – not just an end to the slave trade – and the employment of the Royal Navy to prevent further slave trading. Cugoano was close to Equiano, and both men clearly worked together on their writing. Along with Sancho they form a triumvirate of African writers whose personal experience of slavery infused abolition with an incalculable force. Their publications were of course utterly different. Sancho was the most polished – poised even, Cugoano a simpler, rougher voice, Equiano the more politically alert and specific. Sancho's remains the most curious volume, not least because it was posthumous, but his letters were important in being able to appeal precisely to the people abolition needed to woo: the educated, propertied and the influential.

The slave trade was ended in 1807 and though slavery survived in the British West Indies for another thirty years, to more and more people it seemed a throwback to a bygone world, a grotesque contrast to contemporary British economic and social values and a stain on the British character. As we have already seen, after finally ending colonial slavery, the British changed tack dramatically, henceforth boasting about their national and communal (with little mention of their role in perfecting slavery in the first place). The culture of anti-slavery thereafter became an element in British dealings with the wider world.

This was far removed from the world of Ignatius Sancho, and the black community of the 1770s and 1780s, a mere two generations earlier. At the time of Sancho's birth, few people questioned the slave system. At the time of his death, it had begun to attract its first serious ethical and economic scrutiny. For much of his life, Sancho lived in a community accustomed to regarding Africans and their slave descendants as mere beasts of burden; destined to be the hewers of wood for the betterment of Europeans. Though he could scarcely have imagined it at the time, Sancho was to become one of the early African voices demanding freedom and equality for blacks scattered throughout the Atlantic diaspora. His life, from slave ship to London shop, provides a reminder of the remarkable upheavals and variety in the life of one African, cast around on both sides of the Atlantic by forces beyond his ken or control. Yet it should also remind us of an alternative world; of Africans demanding their freedom, of rising against the odds, of seeking help and comfort among fellow blacks-and forging important links with sympathetic local whites. From such small, apparently insignificant events were laid the foundations for the ultimate dissolution of Britain's mighty slave empire. As he wrote his rather grandiloquent letters, Sancho could hardly have imagined the importance we would later attach to his words.

11 The slave empire and the Age of Revolution

Whereas in the 1780s the black presence had been noisy and unavoidable – registering itself in tract literature, in graphic satire and fashionable portraiture (and ultimately in black writing) – the 1790s were marked by a puzzling silence (with the striking exception of Equiano's work). In the years when the ferment of radical and critical politics shook the structure of the British state (notwithstanding its successful, swift reassertion of control and dominance), the black community – cause and occasion of so much dispute a short while earlier – effectively disappeared from political and social view. There was in effect a muting of the black presence in the era of revolution. What had happened?

The explanation lies in that unfolding of events in France, thence across Western Europe, and the convulsions in the West Indies prompted by the uprising in St Domingue (Haiti). The revolutionary upheavals after 1789 were fundamental and global, and the British state soon found itself locked in a struggle with revolutionary France which, at once, threatened the very security of Britain yet, if won, offered remarkable colonial bounty. There seemed every prospect that the British might acquire French slave colonies in the West Indies which had proved so stunningly lucrative over the past half-century. In that decade of war and confusion, with so much to lose and gain, with whole empires at stake, British statesmen and political commentators could be forgiven for ignoring a small, local problem, i. e. the British black community.

When in the last years of his life, Equiano criss-crossed the country promoting various editions of his autobiography, writing to friends and abolitionists, urging them to promote the end of the slave trade (and to buy his book), he failed to mention the broader revolutionary upheavals in France or in Haiti. His book was as important for its silences and omissions, as for the issues it discussed. Yet it seems curious that the most famous ex-slave in England, agitating for abolition and promoting the virtues of a different relationship with Africa,[1] failed to discuss the events in the Caribbean. Equiano's silence provides us with an important clue to the retreat of the British black community from the public eye in the 1790s. They – and the campaign for abolition which became closely associated with them – withdrew from view in the face of a political (and social) hostility which transmuted the merest hint of reform into Jacobinism.[2] More than that, the war which engulfed the British nation after 1793 was not merely a war versus a continental enemy. It was a war fought in, and for, Caribbean islands. The slave colonies were prized possessions, both for France and the British, and there were enormous strategic and economic gains to be had from naval or land-based victories in the West Indies. The exigencies of war thus quickly rode rough shod over the arguments, widely promoted in the late 1780s, that Britain should re-think its attitude towards black humanity and should move towards the abolition of the slave trade.[3]

There seem to have been two forces which served to render the British black community invisible in the decade of revolution. Firstly, the language of equality – the concept of the rights of man which sustained a growing body of abolitionist sentiment before 1789 – was silenced by the reaction against the excesses of revolutionary France, and the threat from French arms. Secondly, doubts about the morality of slavery were also relegated by the struggle against the French for control of the sea lanes to and from the West Indies, and for control over the islands. Put simply, when tens of thousands of British sailors and soldiers were locked in combat in the Caribbean, it seemed inappropriate – unpatriotic even – to challenge the institution of slavery. It was all too obvious, to anyone watching the course of events in Haiti, what might happen if the British followed the French and dropped their guard over the slaves in the name of a general sentiment of abolition or pro-slavery. By the mid-1790s it was as if Haiti confirmed what planters throughout the region had said since time out of mind; slaves needed permanent and firm control, and any inattention would be punished by a ferocious slave reaction. Haiti seemed to show that the planters had been right all along – in this respect at least. Dropping the plantocratic guard, making concessions to slaves, allowing slaves to listen to the political debates lapping westwards from Europe about rights and representations – all this was guaranteed to prompt slave resistance, and worse.

The end result was that the question of abolition effectively vanished from the political screen after 1792, though there were residual efforts to end the slave trade in Parliament up to 1796. In the previous decade, slavery had been established as a major topic of political debate. In large part this was because of the efforts of the Quakers whose remarkable networks were ideally suited to the task of promoting the anti-slavery message.[4] They had a network which was genuinely national, reaching across the country to form a web of Friends from one town to another, all of whom were sensitized to the question of slavery by earlier Quaker pronouncements and prohibitions against slavery.[5] Moreover, the culture of Quakers was highly literate. From their mid-seventeenth-century origins onwards, no other sect produced such volumes of printed material. And no other sects placed such reliance on literacy and informed discussion as a basis of their culture. Quakers were also remarkably successful business people and had the material wherewithal to fund their chosen printed or political campaigns. Thus it was that the Quaker impact on the initial anti-slavery campaign was out of all proportion to their numbers. But they were shy of overt political activity. Throughout the eighteenth and early nineteenth-century British Quakers kept a deliberately low political profile, (in part because they were denied access to formal office) and sought to operate more as a pressure group on moral issues (slavery, prison reform, the poor). They avoided open political controversy (not least because they had endured more than their fair share of controversy and its associated sufferings in their early days in the mid-seventeenth century). What happened after 1791 was the stuff of Quaker nightmares.

Quakers had attached themselves to the politics of abolition from 1783 onwards. And few could have been in any doubt that Quakers were the most prominent group behind the initial abolition campaign. But, after 1792, abolition became an issue of fierce political contention. Whereas in the mid-1780s it seemed to occupy the moral high-ground, now it was locked into the debate about revolution, slavery and French ideology. For Quakers a period of silence – of quietism – was called for. And to make the Quaker position more difficult still, the country had slid into another war with the French, itself a blow to a fundamental Quaker principle (of non-violence).

One of the Quakers' allies was Equiano. He moved with ease in their circles, had led a deputation of fellow London-based Africans to the main Quaker London meeting,[6] and Quaker backing had clearly been important in securing Equiano's role as commissary to the Sierra Leone scheme in 1787. But when, in the 1790s, Equiano continued his anti-slavery campaign, he did so alone, with no formal organizational support whether from Quakers or from other abolitionist sympathizers. Throughout the years 1792-1797 Equiano was in effect a one-man public anti-slavery campaign when most others had withdrawn. The political climate had changed. Anti-slavery was ill-suited to the new climate of war with France and with the need to sustain (and even expand) the British presence in the Caribbean. Hence, Equiano, criss-crossed the country promoting and selling his autobiography alone.

There were other reasons for his lonely abolitionist stance however. Equiano had published his own book and was making a decent living selling the book through his own promotional efforts. In this he was merely continuing what he had always been good at; an Igbo higgler, keen to make a few pennies wherever the opportunity presented itself. From his earliest days – as a youthful slave in England, on British ships and in the West Indies – Equiano had made money. Making only a few pennies at a time initially, it proved the habit of a lifetime and secured him his freedom in 1766. Throughout his life Equiano had an eye for money-making. In the wake of the Sierra Leone fiasco, he decided the time was right to publish an autobiography which would, at once, be a personal statement and a contribution to abolition. The obvious thing to do would have been to ask the Quakers to back or subsidize the book (they had, after all, financed most anti-slavery tracts so far). But in the event Equiano raised the money via subscriptions, and kept the profits for himself, sinking them into subsequent editions (running to nine before his death in 1797). He also chose to promote the book personally. To do that he spent much of the time between 1789-1797 travelling across Britain promoting his book and speaking to local people and groups about the book and about abolition. He had a ready-made network of abolitionist sympathizers and of Quaker contacts; he was never short of a bed or of a local individual or group to use as a base for his book-promotion. The end result was that his autobiography became something of a best-seller.

It was a curiosity for any number of reasons. Firstly of course for the most obvious of reasons. Here was an African – an ex-slave – promoting a highly sophisticated book filled with literary and biblical allusions; it had the style and substance of literary accomplishment which few contemporaries would expect of an African. Of course that was part of Equiano's aim; to disabuse his British readership of any lingering ideas they might hold about the nature and basis of African life. Equiano presented himself as a man of sensibility; an educated, devout man who had made his way in the world despite remarkable odds and who showed what might be achieved once the restraints of slavery had been removed. And of course, we need to be aware of this subtext when reading Equiano's *Narrative*. He was aiming at a particular market, using a particular tone and purpose, but he was also intent on making money. It was a perfect arrangement for Equiano. He made a profit while at the same time promoting the cause of abolition and anti-slavery. How much influence his book had in the course of the 1790s remains unclear.

Equiano managed to sell large numbers of books. He received a warm welcome wherever he travelled, from Devon to Scotland, from the Hull to Ireland. But what *impact* did his book have? When in 1808 Thomas Clarkson set out to describe the intellectual and literary precursors of abolition he simply failed to mention Equiano. Of course Clarkson was just the first in a long tradition seeking to locate the centre – the cause – of abolition securely in British literary or religious terms. But it is important that Clarkson simply did not recognize Equiano's work, or mention its influence on the course of abolition.[7] And this lends support to this argument.

By the time Equiano's book had begun to sell in numbers, the worries about France had started to multiply. Even the most outspoken of parliamentary spokesmen – led by Wilberforce – were increasingly unhappy. The darkening shadow of the revolution, and, after 1791, the events in Haiti, simply rendered arguments about abolition superfluous at best, dangerous at worst. As news from Haiti worsened for the Europeans, parliamentary abolitionists came under growing pressure simply to drop or postpone abolition. Equally worrying was the fact that the popular radical societies had from 1791 firmly linked their own demands for British political reform to the broader and earlier campaign against the slave trade.[8] But even then the issue of abolition quickly faded as a major issue within the literature spawned by the radical movement of the 1790s.[9] Wilberforce and his parliamentary friends, and abolitionists across the country were unhappy to find themselves linked to a strain of popular radicalism which was ideologically too sympathetic to the French and which spoke too plebeian an accent for their propertied comfort.

The convulsions prompted by the ideals of 1789, and pushed forward by events in Paris, were to send shock waves along the whole West Indian island chain, with tremors felt in Europe. It is clear enough, looking back, why this should have been so. Firstly, few doubted the importance of the islands to British well-being and to her continuing pre-eminence in the Atlantic world. Secondly, the numbers of men flung into the jaws of the West Indian upheavals in the 1790s were enormous – with all the obvious consequences in Britain. The Caribbean was the focus for unprecedented clashes in the 1790s, between the French the British and the Spanish – a major European war in exile – but it was also a unique social and racial clash, beginning in Haiti, but threatening to spill outwards and to engulf every slave island in the region.

The work of David Geggus in particular has helped to redefine what we mean by the `age of revolution'. There was, quite simply, a contagion of revolution, of violence and social instability, which went well beyond the confines of France and her European neighbours. In the process, it was important for the British (or the French) to hang on to their established positions in the Caribbean and not to succumb to their European opponents. Moreover all European colonial powers came to appreciate the point which planters everywhere had asserted for generations past; they must *not* loosen their grip over the slaves. Haiti was, then, a major strategic and economic test for Europe's slaving nations; an example of what could be gained – and what could be lost. In the drive to secure their respective positions in the islands, the Europeans invested millions of pounds and tens of thousands of lives. It proved an epic struggle which utterly overshadowed any minor domestic issue, about slavery at home, or the problems facing black minorities in London. The British black community was rendered insignificant by dint of major problems on the other side of the Atlantic.

The British entered war with France with high hopes of military success. After all, France seemed to be in a tail-spin of collapse and disorder, its empire offering a tempting prize to an expansionist Britain keen to advance its own imperial interests. From the first, the British sought to destroy French naval power – and to expand their own.[10] The main aim of Pitt's war strategy was to seize French West Indian possessions – none more tempting than St Domingue (whose foreign trade in the 1780s outstripped the United States). The French Caribbean was the key to much French prosperity; the islands generated two fifths of the country's foreign trade, two thirds of its ocean-going tonnage, and one third of its seamen. British success would, then, seriously wound the French fiscal state, expand British commercial activity and secure British naval dominance.[11] It was a hugely tempting prospect. The British reckoned however, without two critical factors; the slaves, and the reverses in the war in Europe and the consequent need to direct arms to Europe and *away* from the West Indies. Whereas the Caribbean had initially seemed France's weak flank, by 1795 the weak flank was British in facing Europe.

In outlining his strategy to West Indian planters in 1794, Pitt promised to hang onto all the West Indian islands in British hands after the war. The war effectively obliged the British government to side with the planters and against the slaves, thus deferring for years the eventual coming of black freedom. But it did more than that. It effectively fissured and dispersed that mood of growing sympathy for blacks which had become so apparent in the British drive for abolition between 1787-1792. To compound this process, the French, faced by disasters in the slave islands, emancipated and armed their slaves in the hope that a black guerrilla army might achieve what French conventional forces had failed to do; i. e. pin down and even defeat the British. By 1795 the British faced slave revolt in Grenada and St Vincent, French success in St Lucia, and Maroon upheavals in Jamaica (their most combustible of islands). There was a real danger that far from gobbling up the French colonies, the British might even lose their own. In the event, a massive force of 32,000 men (the biggest overseas expedition to date) was dispatched from Britain to the West Indies in the autumn of 1795. Though it succeeded in restoring British control in critical regions, more than one half of the expedition died (mainly of disease – especially in the quagmire of St Domingue). The rich prospects of securing St Domingue in particular had proved a disastrous illusion, its internal upheavals, the rise of a free black army and the effect of disease devouring a whole British army on an unprecedented scale.

As bad – or at least as threatening – as these huge losses was the contagion of unrest which swept through the slave islands. War, insurrections, rebellion, invasion – all and more leapfrogged from one island to another, threatening a reprise of the social collapse of St Domingue. Jamaica – the centre-piece of the British slave islands – seemed especially vulnerable. Jamaican slaves were notoriously volatile, their owners and masters no less infamous for the grinding nature of their slave-management. With rebellious Maroons at the heart of the island, Jamaica seemed poised to join the list of slave societies destabilized by the contagion of unrest which lapped east and west from St Domingue.

It was vital then that the British maintain their hold in the West Indies, first against the French and then against the slave-based unrest which seeped through the cracks of plantocratic and colonial control. And the British could only secure their strategic hold in and around the islands, by tightening their grip over the slaves. It was an inevitable consequence of the war which raged across the region, in the Atlantic, in Europe and Asia. Yet it also involved an ironic shift, because, on the eve of the Revolution, the British, including a number of ministers who now found themselves master-minding the pro-planter, anti-slave policy, had been wooed to the side of abolition. Again, arguments about abolition – the tone of outraged sympathy for slaves in the West Indies and for the black poor at home – seemed irrelevant in wartime. Moreover this was no ordinary war against a conventional enemy. The French had unleashed on the British a mix of conventional war, guerrilla warfare and a convulsion of racial upheavals. There had, quite simply, been nothing like it before.[12]

The cost to the British had been enormous. In order to expand the empire – but, in the event, to defend what they had – the British had about 89,000 soldiers in the region (something like one half of them died) in addition to between 19-24,000 men at sea. Not surprisingly the debate which these losses prompted in Britain sought a scapegoat, and as one account after another described the suffering of the men involved, the blame for the catastrophic losses fell on the slaves and the hostile environment. It had been a military suffering on a scale the

British had not experienced before and which they were unwilling to contemplate again (at least in the Caribbean).

To compound these worries from the West Indies were the stories – and rumours – of the savagery which the freed slaves in St Domingue had unleashed on those around them. It is, of course, an ironic twist to the story of slave life that the ex-slaves should, quite suddenly, become famous as the *perpetrators* of violence. Notwithstanding the levels of blood-letting and vengeful killings which marked the Haitian upheavals, this concentration on black violence served to deflect attention from one area of progress which abolitionist had made before 1789, namely their account of the endemic violence of the slave system itself. By the mid-1790s onwards however, the violence which preyed on the British mind was black violence.

In many respects it was a reversion to type; a revival of a range of cultural ideas, located in much older images of Africa and Africans, about violence, savagery and `primitive' levels of society. It was also as if the planters had been proved correct. They had, from the first, warned that should they drop their plantocratic guard for a moment, the slaves would immediately revert to their natural African `savagery'. Yet the arguments were not all on one side. It was possible, when considering the success of black resistance under the leadership of Toussaint, to see a challenge to traditional views about white dominance. Here, after all, was a black army which had destroyed military invaders from the two most powerful nations in Europe (albeit with a great deal of assistance from sickness).[13] Equally, as Michael Duffy has pointed out, the British recruitment of twelve black regiments for the regular army, as a response to French military recruitment of slaves, suggests a more benign view of black potential. Yet it was as much a measure of desperation, forced on the British government (against fierce colonial and planter opposition) because there were simply not enough white troops for the task of containing the French, let alone the slaves. Though these black troops may well have proved their worth, their enlistment was more an act of military necessity than a concession to a more tolerant, benign view of race. The events in Haiti – the victories, the losses – had hardened British arteries against slaves everywhere.

It is hard, looking back from the late 1790s, to see any sign that events had been anything but a serious set-back for those who had embarked, a few years before, to assert the rights of man – black and white – and to demand an end to the Atlantic slave trade. The exigencies of war, and the losses in Haiti simply rode rough-shod over whatever progress had been made in Britain towards a more egalitarian view of mankind.

What, in the meantime, had happened to the British black community? What had happened to that small, primarily metropolitan gathering of black people who had been the centre of such interest and concern on the eve of the revolution? In many respects it survived much as before. Recent research on parish, criminal and charitable records – allied to the early census data – shows that the black population was tiny (never forming more than 0. 55% of the total population of

London), though other blacks of course lived in Bristol and Liverpool. It was overwhelmingly male, it was poor and it was consequently over-represented in the criminal statistics.[14]

These bare statistics of the black community are confirmed by contemporary iconography. Whenever an artist or cartoonist wished to portray contemporary poverty or plebeian lewdness (sexuality below stairs, bar-room drunken excess) there we will find images of contemporary blacks. Though Hogarth used black images in more than two dozens of his pictures, he often inverted the conventional relationships between black and white, with hints of sympathy or implied criticisms of whites.[15] In two of Isaac Cruikshanks watercolours from the 1790s, his images of London blacks confirm the realities of black plebeian life. One, *Foot Pad's – Or much ado about Nothing* (1795), shows a black woman aiding a highway robbery, on the outskirts of London. The other, of 1792, shows a black trying to sell rotten meat to a fashionable lady, with suggestions of sexual sauciness in the black's response.[16]

This visual evidence continued into the nineteenth century and confirms what we know already from other sources The black community was poor. Those who managed to find employment worked as servants or as sailors (hence the concentration of blacks in dockside parishes). It is also clear that blacks were the object of confusing responses by local whites. It is all-too-easy to imagine that, throughout the 1780' and 1790s, British-based blacks were the victim solely of derision and hostility. Of course such animosity existed in abundance, and be gauged from the letters of Sancho in 1782, through to the tract warfare between abolitionists and West Indians from the mid-1780s, to acts of individual aggression and violence. At its worst, it took the form of cavalier cheating and aggression. Equiano had to be permanently on his guard against being cheated in his various commercial ventures; whites knew that blacks were unlikely to secure legal support in any dispute with whites. Similarly, and despite the 1772 Mansfield judgement, violations of black rights continued, with individuals threatened with kidnap and enforced return to the West Indies against their will.[17] Yet this formed only one part of the story and we might return to the experience of Equiano himself to round off the picture.

When Equiano travelled throughout the country promoting and selling his book in the 1790s, he stayed with friends and acquaintances. He seems never to have had trouble securing accommodation among British friends – both high and low. He lodged with a shoemaker in London and with more prosperous men in other cities. Men of reforming sensibility went out of their way to provide him with letters of support and recommendation, confirming his stalwart qualities and virtues. He had, in brief, a wide range of British friends and associates who were keen to help and support him, and to help find him friends and accommodation elsewhere, and to support the sale of his autobiography in very personal ways.[18] Yet this same man, Equiano, had been periodically brutalized in England by other contemporaries. He had been re-enslaved on the Thames and shipped back to the West Indies against his will, he had been regularly cheated of money and possessions. There is no reason to think that Equiano's experience was different from other black contemporaries. And yet, in the 1790s, the very time when events in Haiti had so blighted British discussion of slavery, Equiano continued to receive friendly and sympathetic treatment across the country.

The rub however is that Equiano *was* different. Here was a man of sensibility; devout, literate, industrious and achieving – the very image of a successful, ex-slave which contemporary whites would appreciate. Equiano quite clearly set out to convey to his readership – and those he met – the *persona* of the devout, self-improving autodidact. Even the frontispiece to his book, showing an elegant portrait of Equiano, dressed in the finest of clothing and (suitably) clutching a Bible, confirmed this overall image. Though he authored the *Narrative* as an African, and throughout the late 1780s and 1790s added variants on the words `the African' to his signature, the image Equiano conveyed was not of the conventional African, nor even of those blacks around him in London. It was an anglicized African; one who spoke in a manner which his British readers would appreciate. It was, in a word, far removed from the Africans of the slave ships and the plantations (though Equiano's tale was about both of those experiences) and it seemed far removed from the poverty and precariousness of life among the black poor in London.

In fact Equiano was much closer to that indigent black experience than we might imagine. He was, until 1787, often unemployed in London, managing to make ends meet through his usual efforts and skills (hairdressing, servant work, seafaring). And it was only the success of his book after 1789 which (along with marriage to an English women in 1792) brought him the material security he had always sought.

Equiano supervised nine different editions of his book before he died in 1797. Yet nowhere did he mention the events unfolding in St Domingue. Here, and elsewhere, his book is striking for a number of notable omissions. He fails for example to mention the Somerset Case (1772), and he overlooks the terrible events of the *Zong* massacre (1782) even though he was instrumental in bring the incident to the attention of Granville Sharp, the best friend to blacks in London.[19] His ignoring of Haiti is however more easily understood, for it was an uncomfortable affair which could hardly have helped his arguments. Here was the African, spokesman for the British black community (a position which remained effectively unchallenged despite the calumnies flung at him by the West India lobby). And his book was not merely an autobiography but an illustration of what could be achieved by an ex-slave. Equiano was a man who had risen from the grimmest of circumstances, who had found God and had effected the life-style of an Englishman. The disasters in the West Indies ran counter to the whole thrust and tone of Equiano's *Narrative*. St Domingue threatened everything Equiano stood for. The violence, licence and mayhem of the slave revolution horrified friends of abolition everywhere. It depressed Wilberforce, alienated the faint-hearted, and effectively put an end to abolition for a decade. Though Equiano was successful as a book-seller, it was hard to maintain the broader sympathies for slaves under the shadow of the Haitian troubles and the consequent loss of British life.

In later editions of his book, Equiano went to pains to describe what would happen if the slave trade to Africa were replaced by a `normal' free trade to Africa. He turned contemporary arguments on their head by claiming that abolition would be good for British trade and manufacture. African produce, African markets for British goods, all and more would combine, under a non-slave trade system, to enhance British material well-being still further. It was a neat – and new – way of turning the West Indian flank. The slave lobby had always argued that the slave system was too valuable, too important to Britain even to countenance any moral tinkering with one aspect of the overall system. End the slave trade, and the fabric of the slave system (and the prosperity which flowed to Britain from that system) would collapse. Equiano turned the argument on its head. Expose Africa to normal trade and both manufacture and trade would, far from being ruined, be greatly enhanced. Haiti effectively jeopardized both this argument and the pro-slave sympathy so assiduously cultivated by abolitionists in the 1780s.

Equiano did not live to see the unfolding of events he had helped to prompt; the revival of abolitionist support a decade later and the final parliamentary passage of abolition in 1806. Furthermore his own contribution was quickly forgotten after his death in 1797. The community which he spoke for, and which he so memorably represented, in print and practise, survived – though in much altered form. It was a community forged as a direct by-product of the slave trade. It was, in effect, just one more aspect of the broader diasporic movement which scattered African people across the Atlantic world and even further afield. It was a community which was sustained by the maritime movement of peoples; slaves back and forth, free blacks in the company of masters and mistresses and, of course, sailors criss-crossing the Atlantic in Royal Naval and merchant vessels.[20] But with the Atlantic slave trade under attack it made no economic sense, from the mid-1780s onwards, to transport slaves *into* Britain as mere social attachments to their owners; they were too valuable to be moved from the slave colonies. Moreover the climate of opinion had changed dramatically in Britain in the course of the 1780s. The culmination of the legal attacks on domestic slavery, the early tract warfare against the slave trade, and the broadly based revulsion against the worst excesses of the slave trade, had served to sour the atmosphere for slave owners in Britain. They could no longer be sure that their black servants – whatever their legal position – would remain at their side. Blacks simply ran away (especially in London) from their owners/employers, often preferring a marginal life among the capital's indigent than to live as domestics in a slave-owners home. Worse still – for the West Indians – British opinion seemed to have shifted against them.

It may still have been true that the value of the slave colonies continued to be widely accepted in Britain. This, after all, was the core argument of the West India lobby from beginning to end; how could the British so much as contemplate ridding itself of such a lucrative source of income and material prosperity? The abolitionists' prime, long-term task was thus to erode that assumption; to cultivate an alternative and contrary view of the islands and their inhabitants. It was easiest to suggest that the cost involved (a cost largely unrecognized by the British – or the West India lobby) was too high a price. The price of course was paid by the slaves, most horribly (and most easily demonstrated) on the slave ships. The abolitionists' first task therefore was to create a revulsion against Atlantic slave trading. And that was quickly and widely effected in the course of the 1780s. To attack West Indian slavery itself was however an altogether different matter, and even before the slave trade had been completely undermined, events in the Caribbean – and Europe – intervened to complicate matters.

The immediate and long-term consequences of the West Indian convulsions were complex. The initial optimism, that the British had the opportunity to snatch the French colonies and thereby deal a mortal blow against French economic and naval power, quickly crumbled into the gory realities of attrition, defeat and debacle. The British were by the mid-1790s, simply hanging onto what they had. But the cost was enormous. Millions of pounds, tens of thousands of men, permanent and universal slave upheaval and discontent, (to say nothing of confronting victorious French arms across the Channel) raised a question which few had asked before. Was it worth it? Were the West Indies *so* valuable that they demanded such investment in lives and money?

It was a question which Equiano had asked, in his own modest way, throughout these same years. His *Narrative* raised the question of an alternative economic future for the Atlantic system. Did trade to and from Africa and the Americas always *have* to hinge on the transfer and the labour of African humanity? Perhaps a freer trade in goods and produce might benefit all sides (and in the process bring `civilization' to Africa itself)?[21] It was of course an argument most effectively advanced in 1776 by Adam Smith. But by the 1790s what we are witnessing is the first crumbling of that broadly based consensus that the economics of the slave system were impregnable. The old certainties were now open to scrutiny and doubt. Previously those certainties were often unspoken because they needed no explanation. It was enough merely to wave a hand in London, Liverpool and Bristol towards the skyline of ships masts and the quaysides of buoyant activity in and around the ships fresh in from, or departing to the West Indies. But the 1790s saw a shift.

Casualties mounted, cost increased – and yet the purpose of those costs (an advance of British slave-based power, a restoration of stability among the slaves) seemed as far away as ever. Ministers began to grumble that perhaps, after all, here was a prize *not* worth the effort. But there was something more imprecise, less easily gauged, about the British reactions to the revolution in Haiti. Throughout the 1780s the abolitionists (and friends of the blacks in general) had made great play about black potential; about what might be achieved if slavery were ended. The consequences of slavery were to be seen in the streets of London, in the form of the black poor, disabled by their enslavement, from securing a decent living.

Slavery could be portrayed as a process of disablement, stripping away the energy and initiative of free people in order to reduce the slaves to an absolute dependency on their masters. We know of course that such an image was deeply flawed, and the West Indian islands had plenty of examples of independent slave activity and energy on the edges of plantation life.[22] However, viewed from London, it seemed a reasonable case, and appeared to find support in the form of the black poor and in the arguments of their spokesmen. Discussion about slavery could focus on black life in London by way of varied (and conflicting) illustrations. From 1772 (in the wake of the Somerset Case) to 1788 (in the aftermath of Sierra Leone) arguments about slaves and slave-trading had, time and again, reverted to examples of blacks *in London*. Here, at home, were illustrations of what the slave system produced. Of course, in reality the experiences of blacks in London threw only *indirect*, pale light on the course of Atlantic slavery. The heart of the slave experience lay not in London – or Bristol – but in the sugar fields of the Caribbean. Yet the black presence served its purpose for early abolitionists – and even for the West India lobby. The miserable fate of the local black poor provided *both* sides with evidence for their arguments. West Indians thought that it showed fundamental black indolence and fecklessness; a reversion to type which no amount of humanitarian good-will could change. Abolitionists (and black spokesmen) on the other hand pointed to the disabling effects of slavery. But such a debate was, in the grand scheme of Atlantic slavery, a form of parish pump politics; concerned about the local and the immediate, when the real issues lay elsewhere. This all became dramatically clear after 1791.

The French and Haitian revolutions, the ebb and flow of slave resistance and white colonial reaction, put British black affairs – the parochial problems of blacks in Britain – in global perspective. The clash that really countered was in the Caribbean And it was, obviously, a clash of titanic proportions; upheavals of peoples and ideals which were to restructure the social and human geography of the region. But the cost of the upheavals of the 1790s could be reduced to a simple question – was it worth it? This question (uttered initially by Ministers who had to count the human and financial costs) was muttered by growing numbers of people in later years. The grand edifice of the British slave system was beginning to crumble.

12 Slavery, the law and slave resistance

Background: the impact of the 1790s

The 1790s proved a decade of major change, not merely in Europe, but in the story of slavery in the Americas. The cataclysmic upheaval in the slave society of St Domingue was unique. It heralded the first independent black republic outside of Africa and was (after the creation of the USA) the second post-colonial society of the modern era. It also formed a turning point in the history of Atlantic slavery, for it set in train a sequence of strategic and military disasters for the Atlantic's leading slave trader – the British. These, in their turn, proved critical in loosening the British attachment to the slave trade, and ultimately to slavery itself. The Haitian revolution (almost completely ignored by an older generation of prominent historians of the `Age of Revolution'.[1]) marked a shift in the history of Atlantic slavery. Despite the work of C. L. R James and his intellectual ward Eric Williams, it has taken a long time for historians to accept the full significance of the events in Haiti.

The course of events in the West Indies in the 1790s have been clearly outlined in recent years.[2] Though the spark which ignited the upheavals in St Domingue came initially from France, and though the vernacular of freedom adopted by black, white and brown in the island were clearly grounded in the French Revolution, the exact nature and course of the slave upheaval had distinctively local – and African – roots. Moreover the events unfolding in Haiti had both immediate and long-tern consequences across the region – and even further afield. The effects of the Haitian revolution were felt throughout slave societies in the Americas. The language of freedom rushed ahead of the fleeing refugees, causing concern and alarm among slave owners everywhere. In the course of the 1790s, no Caribbean planter could feel comfortable, with ideas about rights and equality floating in and out of local discussions, among whites but, more corrosively among their slaves.

There was a veritable *contagion* of equality which sent French ideals lapping island to island. And to add to the planters' problems, large number of people, black and white, fled the Haitian upheavals for the safety of other islands and mainland America. At first however the British regarded the Haitian revolution as a tempting opportunity to expand their slave interests. If they could seize the French colony they would add the most lucrative of West Indian islands to their collection and, at a stroke, remove the commercial threat which Haiti had come to pose to British sugar production. Pitt's government dispatched an army to take Haiti – but it, like the French military in the island, was slowly devoured by that potent mix of insurrectionary slave arms and virulent local disease. British ambition crumbled in the teeth of defeat and diseased debacle. Tens of thousands of men died, millions of pounds were wasted, and all for what? Disruptive ideas about freedom and equality, and practical dangers continued to flow through the region, and yet, by the mid 1790s, the British had nothing to show for their efforts and cost. The question was raised; was it worth it? Were the slave islands *so* valuable that they warranted such disastrous losses?

The British Ministers, whose decision to dispatch an army to seize Haiti had proved so costly, also began to ask that question. In fact, the question had *already* been raised, more than a decade earlier, by a small band of British abolitionists and philanthropists. The disasters in Haiti brought centre stage a debate about slavery (its value, morality and legality) which had been simmering in Britain for some years past. The clashes in the Caribbean were of huge proportions; between black and white, slave and free, empire and freedom. By the mid-1790s the cost of their disastrous involvement in Haiti to the British, raised a simple question which had already been posed by abolitionists; was it worth it? Nor was this question merely a question of strategy or accountancy; the counting of global advantage and disadvantage, or the totting up of losses and gains. At heart, the question touched on a string of related moral and ethical issues about black slavery, issues which had been largely overlooked by the sheer material abundance disgorged by the slave societies of the Americas. The Haitian upheaval allowed ever more people to question the course of events in the Caribbean (also in Africa and on the high seas). By the mid-1790s, what they saw there caused them growing unease.

Slavery and the law

The importance of Atlantic slavery to the development of the modern western world is no longer in doubt, though arguments continue about the precise economic calibration of that importance. We know that the British did not initiate Atlantic slavery, but, from the late seventeenth century onwards, they perfected it. The British enslavement of Africans, the nature, volume and speed of British oceanic transportations, the remarkable well-being disgorged by the British slave societies in the islands and in mainland America, the domestic British entanglement with slavery (finance, commerce, insurance, shipping, ports) – all and more speak to a hugely important intimacy between Britain and slavery in the Americas.

Slaves, and the produce they cultivated, made their presence felt throughout British (and European) life.[3] Though it was comforting for the British to imagine that slavery was out of sight (at the far edge of Atlantic shipping routes) and therefore out of mind, the development of the Atlantic economy threw up unavoidable confrontations with slavery; confrontations which took place not in Africa, at sea or in the colonies, but at home, in Britain. As the Atlantic slave economy developed, with its massive movements of peoples across the Atlantic, the influence of slavery intruded itself ever more closely into British domestic life.

Firstly – and most obviously – were the slaves cast ashore in Britain – the human ebb and flow of the Atlantic system. Their presence raised a number of issues for domestic British life, most notably, the legality of slavery in England (and Scotland). From the late seventeenth century onwards, a variety of English courts had to confront the question of whether slavery was legal in England? And if so, on what basis?

Europeans developed their slave systems in the Americas at a time when slavery in Western Europe was in decline. Moreover the nature of black chattel slavery which emerged in the Americas was quite different from the forms of bondage which had characterized, for example, medieval feudalism.[4] In the British case, the colonizing state had had a direct (and continuing) role in how slavery emerged on the far side of the Atlantic. From the first, the state had played a determining role in the slave colonies; in devising colonizing schemes, in granting licenses, consolidating funds, encouraging settlers and invasions; all and more received seals of royal (and Cromwellian) approval. More than that, Parliament was actively involved. A variety of Parliamentary Acts – most notably the Navigation Acts which authorized and monitored English Atlantic slave trading – helped to sanction the movement of Africans across the Atlantic. Even when the slave colonies were securely established, the King-in-Parliament continued to monitor affairs in the islands; colonial legislation was referred to London for approval and alteration. There was, then, no doubt that slavery as it thrived in the eighteenth-century British West Indies (and North America) had been encouraged and directed by London, quite apart from the role played by particular economic vested interests, in London and the slaving ports, in fashioning New World slavery.

How the slaves in the colonies saw the process of slave law was of course quite different. The laws governing slavery took the form of its most violent and oppressive expression: the legal corporal punishment and executions of errant slaves. Of course to most slaves this may have seemed no more than another, albeit extreme, variant on daily life; where white owners (mainly masters) were able to secure their wishes through the exercise of brute force, punishing back-sliding and shortcomings by violence, often on a grim scale.

Owners of slaves in Britain were not able to treat their slaves in so capriciously violent a fashion. The black community in Britain was primarily male and poor (hence finding its intimate friendships with poor white women), it was concentrated close to the water's edge in London (or in fashionable homes) and much of it was, initially, enslaved. Not surprisingly, we find a spectrum of experiences within the black community ranging from Equiano and Ignatius Sancho through to anonymous beggars and crossing sweepers. As the eighteenth century progressed, more blacks arrived, prompting acerbic remarks from the West India lobby – planters and their scribes – who disliked the sight of blacks in Britain (but who had been responsible for the migration of many of them in the first place). What worried some of the slave owners – apart from the prospect of losing their enslaved domestics to the lure of a growing free black community – was the corrosive effect black freedom might have on their ability to deal with slaves as they saw fit. Most troubling of all however was the legal threat to curb their ability to take slaves *back* to the Americas, or sell them to outward-bound vessels.

English courts in the course of the eighteenth century rehearsed a number of issues thrown up by the enslaved black presence in England. Were slaves freed simply by stepping ashore in England? Were they free once baptized? Could they be removed abroad against their wishes? These ruminations culminated in the celebrated 1772 Somerset Case which, despite a series of confusions (then and since) clearly put an end to the practice of forcible removal. The consequences were far-reaching. Over the next twelve years, fifteen masters tried to uphold their legal right over slaves in English courts; all failed. The nub of the 1772 decision was that slavery had been outlawed (even though we know of examples where blacks continued to be held and treated as slaves *after* 1772).[5] It also had a much deeper significance, for it exposed the contradictions at the very heart of the slave system. The British derived abundant (and increasing) wealth from its Atlantic slave empire. Yet, in 1772, the English Lord Chief Justice had determined that blacks in Britain were guaranteed certain rights as residents in England. When did those rights stop – and where did they begin? Were they applicable on British ships – or just within British waters? For the planters however Somerset posed a more worrying issue. The legal debates culminating in the 1772 decision had hinged on discussions about the *humanity* of the blacks involved. The slave ships and the slave colonies operated on an utterly different principle; that slaves were chattels and goods, items of trade and commerce to be sold, bought, bequeathed and inherited like other inanimate objects. This was of course a new variant on the much older debate described so brilliantly by David Brion Davis as *The Problem of Slavery in Western Culture*.[6]

But what did all this mean to the slaves, locked in their daily routines, in the slave colonies? Their own responses to slavery were of an altogether more troubling nature.

Slave resistance

Slaves resisted their bondage from first to last. Not all slaves of course, but enough to ensure that control remained a persistent and recurring problem for those in charge of slaves. Within Africa, on the slave ships and on the slave properties of the Americas, slave resistance was an everyday feature of local life. There is however a danger here. In recent years there has been a tendency to see in each and every slave reaction a manifestation of a broader culture of slave resistance. If everything slaves did was a form of resistance, the concept becomes meaningless. We need to adopt a more subtle approach to slave resistance.

Slave culture emerged as a balancing act: knowing how to balance slave interests and needs against the imperatives of obedience and industry. Knowing what they could get away with and when were important lessons learned by every growing slave, and by every African who survived to reach the Americas. Footdragging, playing dumb, feigning ignorance, going slow – all and more became persistent complaints among slave owners everywhere. They also formed the basis for the ubiquitous belief, in white societies on both sides of the Atlantic, in black indolence and stupidity. In its turn this belief became a central plank in the plantocratic defence of slavery; only the constraints of slavery would keep blacks at work. Remove the compulsion, the threats, the violence, and blacks would revert to their `natural' type – of feckless indolence and stupidity.

Yet slaves also had good reason not to push their footdragging resistance too far. Like all forms of resistance, it contained real dangers for slaves. Again, part of all slaves' upbringing was to learn how far they could go; which boundaries could not be crossed with impunity. Even so, time and again, slaves *did* cross those boundaries, regularly and in large numbers. They ran away, though we now know that they tended to run away *to* rather then *from* people: to loved ones rather than away from objects of tyranny. They damaged goods, produce and animals; they cussed and answered back. Sometimes, of course, they reared up in frustration and anger. The dangers were obvious, and the penalties generally fearful. Best known of all, were the incidents when slaves erupted in bouts of volcanic fury, never more devastating than in Haiti. But long before the French slave upheavals, slaves in the British islands, especially in Jamaica, had been characterized by violent resistance. There and elsewhere, slaves paid for their overt forms of resistance (striking a white person, incendiarism, individual or communal violence) through sufferings which seemed progressively more barbaric as the eighteenth century advanced. What may have seemed tolerable as a means of containing slaves in, say, the early days of seventeenth-century settlement, seemed archaic and wrong by the early nineteenth century. While the western world was changing, reshaped by ideals of enlightenment and reformed sensibility, the planters' world remained unreconstructed; addicted to violence as the main way of sustaining slavery itself. Again, the question began to be asked; was it worth it?

Slave resistance was then endemic to slavery in the British slave colonies. The difficulty, now, it to draft a more nuanced interpretation of resistance than many historians have accepted so far. It is also becoming clearer, notably from the work of Africanists, that African experiences may well have played a critical role in shaping the more violent and turbulent slave responses in the Americas. Put simply, the most violent of slave reactions may have been rooted in *African* experiences of violence and warfare. But we need also to ask; what did slave resistance achieve?

In some ways the question may seem inappropriate, for a great deal of slave resistance was a reflex reaction; spontaneous outbursts which had no grand aim. In the cases of unsuccessful violent resistance, it seems clear enough that the repression which inevitably followed unsuccessful slave resistance involved a *tightening* of control over the slaves. Slave violence convinced slave owners that force and tight control alone could answer their needs. Yet, in the British case, slaves seemed to resort to more violent solutions *at the very time* when Britain itself was rethinking its attitude towards slavery. Indeed the abolitionist campaigns from 1787 onwards were shaped around an attachment to a peaceful process of political change; persuading Parliament of the need to implement abolitionist measures. Here we see the British attachment to the due process of law as the critical means of transforming slavery. Yet, to repeat, in precisely these years, slaves in the British West Indies began to take matters into their own hands.

Rumours of the abolitionist agitation in Britain to end the slave trade had percolated into the slave quarters by the late eighteenth century. This was not surprising. Firstly, in the initial agitation, in the 1780s, there were Africans and other ex-slaves in London who were active in the first abolitionist movement, and who had friends and contacts on both sides of the Atlantic. Equiano for one moved with ease in black society in England, in North America and in the slave societies of the Caribbean. There were large numbers of blacks working at sea on the armada of British vessels criss-crossing the Atlantic. Inevitably they carried news and gossip, greetings and help from one black group to another. More potent still perhaps was the life-style of West Indian whites. Surrounded by domestic slaves, whites found their every word – especially at table and in moments of social ease – quickly carried back to the kitchens and thence to the slave quarters. Quite simply, slaves in the islands knew a great deal about the political comings and goings both in the islands and, in a more garbled form, in London. But whatever its form, the enslaved awareness of the changing political climate in Britain formed the backcloth for the troubles which erupted in the islands in the early nineteenth century.

Rebellions

The British slave colonies were disturbed by three major slave uprising in the early nineteenth century; Barbados (1816), Demerara (1823) and, worst of all, Jamaica (1831-32). From the complexity of causes, two critical factors stand out. Firstly the shifts in slave demography brought about by the ending of the slave trade in 1807, and secondly the work of the early Christian missionaries.

In the wake of abolition, planters were denied access to fresh supplies of Africans – the very lifeblood of the islands from the early days. They were consequently obliged to rejig their labour management. This had repercussions for large numbers of slaves who might reasonably have expected to expect to be able to improve themselves. Slaves once destined for better jobs now found themselves thrust backwards, into the harsh work of the field gangs; i. e. to do the work once reserved primarily for Africans.

More potent still however was the influence of Christianity. From the first – despite their protestations that they were beacons of Christian civility in a sea of slave darkness – planters in the British West Indies had persistently denied slaves access to Christianity. The churches, especially the Anglican church, had been loathe to intrude. But from the late eighteenth century, the rise of new nonconformist groups, (notably the Baptists and Methodists) determined to evangelize more vigorously. Chapels and peripatetic preachers began to swarm over the slave islands, converting thousands, encouraging black preachers, introducing the Bible and providing an ideology which slaves could use to their own ends. The impact was dramatic. However devout, however Christian the slaves became, what slaves took from their new Christian experience had profound consequences for slave society.

They accepted that salvation could be theirs. There was a master – a God – who outranked their own immediate owners. The imagery of Christ's suffering and ultimate salvation seemed to parallel their own miserable fate. And they were able to listen, in ever growing crowds, to black preachers. Here we find auto-didactic slaves preaching of heaven and salvation, in locations well away from the plantation. We even know of slaves elbowing aside whites to secure a pew in church. The world was slowly turning upside down – and all within the apparently innocent context of a nonconformity which, in Britain, has long been regarded as conservative. In the slave islands, its impact was utterly different and disruptive.

There were of course other, local, more specific sparks, behind the great slave upheavals in Barbados, Demerara, and Jamaica. Though not on the scale of the Haitian uprising, the violence and blood-letting was grim enough. Jamaica – true to its violent traditions – was worst of all. Hundreds dead (killed or executed) with millions of pounds worth of damage, this last slave revolt, at the very time Parliament was addressing the issue of black freedom, proved the last straw. The question first raised in the troubled years of the 1790s once again swirled around British politics; was it worth it?

Abolition and amnesia

Britain in 1830 was a different society from that of the 1790s. The post-war dislocations and unrest at home, the development of a new radical politics and rising demands for social and political change had served to change the political culture. But there was a deeper, more fundamental transformation in *sensibility*, which was partly rooted in Enlightenment ideas but more especially in the dissemination of evangelicalism. Old cultural habits found themselves under growing scrutiny and complaint. The traditional attachment to violent, bloody sports and pleasure, the inhumanities against the mentally troubled, the errant and animals – all and more came under attack. So too did slavery.

Slavery was in effect one of the major, unreconstructed institutions of the *ancien regime*; a throw-back (for all its unquestioned material well-being) to an old world which seemed ever more out of kilter with the early nineteenth century. To a society attached to a belief in progress, here was an institution rooted in old habits which seemed ill-suited to the modern world. Highly protected (when economic convention demanded free-trade), grossly violent (when violence was increasingly disliked) costly (in local and imperial investment, at a time when the public purse was closely guarded). To repeat, the problem of British slavery could be distilled to a simple question; was it worth it?

In the rising chorus of objections to slavery in the 1820s, the abolition movement developed a remarkably popular constituency (among working people, among women – quite apart from the traditionally active propertied). Abolition became popular. It is also clear, from recent analysis of the abolitionists words and petitions, and from studying their organizational bases, that the bedrock of abolition was religious. Much of the language of abolition was couched in religious terms, the bulk of anti-slavery agitation emerged from churches, chapels or from the activities of devout abolitionists. Of course the context had changed. The economics of slavery were under scrutiny as never before, not least because the major slave-grown crops could be secured, perhaps more cheaply, from other regions of the world. The West India lobby was also fatally weakened by its insistence on its traditional, bloody methods of maintaining slavery, by the rise of other sugar cultivations, by the changing political and humane culture in Britain and by the picador activities of a zealous anti-slavery movement across the face of Britain.

Like abolition of the slave trade in 1807, the end of slavery was effected by an Act of Parliament. Similarly the massive compensation (a staggering £20 million) paid to the slave owners was a parliamentary decision. Why not pay it to the slaves, some abolitionists argued? Black freedom was greeted in Britain as a triumph for Christian morality over a self-serving, cruel and immoral economic system. Thereafter the British embarked on that nineteenth-century crusade against slavery the world over; in Africa, in India and Asia. The slaving poacher had seen the light and became the abolitionist game keeper. This triumph of British abolition and its much heralded achievements have, ever since, created a smoke-screen between British slavery and British abolition. There has been a historiographical tradition (which survives to this day) which prefers to look to abolition rather than Britain's slaving past. Yet in the century *before* abolition, the British had shipped almost three millions Africans across the Atlantic. Despite the enormity of Britain's slaving role, despite the unquestioned ramifications of slavery in Britain itself (from its communal sweet tooth through to its merchant and commercial benefits), the public memory is more likely to recall Wilberforce and his friends than the evidence of slave trading.

The slave empire which the British orchestrated in the Americas was critical both in colonial and in domestic British experience from the mid seventeenth to the mid-nineteenth centuries. Some British historians however continue to write as if slavery was a mere noise of stage; a peripheral issue, on the far side of the Atlantic, of passing and marginal interest to domestic life. The difficulty facing historians remains, of course, that black slavery was an institution fashioned *for* the

Americas. The slaves were on the other side of the Atlantic. Yet slavery was conceived, developed and brought to perfection by *Europeans*, in exile in the Americas but also in Europe's major trading ports and mercantile centres. Moreover, from an early date slavery found a domestic setting in Britain itself (though admittedly on a small scale.) Slavery was paraded in English courts, it was an important concern of Parliament and Government. It was also of immediate concern to the British fiscal state and, of course, to its broader strategic interests. Slavery was kept in place by Britain's growing military might. The Royal Navy protected British sea routes, defended the slave islands and ensured that Britain's distant slave interests progressed as peaceably as possible. Great swathes of the British domestic economy were locked into the slave system, most noticeably of course in the slaving ports and in London. Slavery was, in brief, very much an issue of domestic British concern and well-being.

The British slave system was shaped and kept in place by the law as much as by the armed might of the British imperial state (and the cavalier violence of the planters). But like all slave systems, it had to contend with – to contain – a slave population for whom resistance had become part of the warp and the weft of everyday life. It is easy to exaggerate that slave resistance, but no slave-owner – or slaving society – could afford to ignore it. Two of the major slave systems of the Americas, in Haiti and the USA, both collapsed in the violent upheavals of war. The British system on the other hand succumbed, ultimately, to the force of law. An Act of Parliament ended the slave trade, and a generation later another Act brought slavery itself to an end. Precisely *why* Parliament turned against both the slave trade and slavery remains a tantalizing problem. But even then, within Parliament, and in the broader national debate which fuelled the abolitionists campaigns (1787-1807 and 1824-1838), it should be clear that slavery was a central issue. Once black freedom came, finally and fully in 1838, Britain's slaving past was instantly consigned to the memory hole. Thereafter, a historical amnesia set in. British historians have much preferred to discuss British abolition rather than British slavery. Britain the abolitionist, rather than Britain the slave trader, became the *leitmotif* for national self-congratulation and public memory. Despite the huge volumes of scholarship on slavery in the past generation, British historians have yet to accept the importance of Atlantic slavery in the shaping of modern Britain.

Notes

Introduction

1 Herbert S. Klein, *The Atlantic Slave Trade,* Cambridge, 1999.

2 David Richardson, 'The British empire and the Atlantic Slave Trade,1660-1807' in *The Oxford History of the British Empire. The Eighteenth Century,* P.J. Marshall, ed., Oxford, 1998. Other essays in this same volume are invaluable for an understanding of British imperial slavery.

3 This was the central argument of course of Eric Williams in his book *Capitalism and Slavery,* 1944. For the latest contribution to this continuing debate see Seymour Drescher, *From Slavery to Freedom,* London, 1999.

4 See for example Frank O'Gorman, *The Long Eighteenth Century. British Political and Social History, 1688-1832,* London, 1997.

5 See essays by Jacob M. Price, Richard B. Sheridan, David Richardson in P.J. Marshall, *Eighteenth Century, op. cit,* and by James Horn, Hilary McD. Beckles and Nuala Zahedieh in *The Origins of Empire,* Nicholas Canny, ed., Oxford, 1998.

6 Michael Craton and James Walvin, *A Jamaican Plantation. Worthy Park, 1760-1970,* London,1970; James Walvin, *Black and White. The Negro and English Society, 1555-1945,* London,1973.

7 More traditional Marxist efforts to provide an intellectual coherence to the world of Atlantic slavery have never fully convinced most students of slavery, though a number of Marxist scholars from C.L.R. James and Eric Williams onwards have proved immensely influential in prompting structural analysis of the Atlantic system.

8 James Walvin, *Making the Black Atlantic,* London, 2000; *An African's Life. The Life and Times of Olaudah Equiano, 1745-1797,* London, 1998; *Fruits of Empire. Exotic Produce and British Taste, 1660-1800,* London, 1997.

Chapter One

1 James Walvin, *An African's Life. The Life and Times of Olaudah Equiano*, London, 1998.

2 Letter of July 27 1766, in Paul Edwards and Polly Rewt, eds, *The Letters of Ignatius Sancho*, Edinburgh, 1994, pp.85-86.

Chapter Two

1 For the latest commentary on abolition, see Seymour Drescher, *From Slavery*, *op.cit.*

2 Philip D.Morgan, 'British Encounters with Africans and African-Americans circa 1600-1780', in *Strangers within the Realm. Cultural Margins of the First British Empire*, Bernard Bailyn and Philip D. Morgan, eds., Chapel Hill and London, 1991, pp.161-162.

3 James Walvin, *Fruits of Empire. Exotic Produce and British Taste, 1660-1800*, London, 1997.

4 For the broader story of the rise of material consumption – of which sugar is a part – see the essays in *Consumption and the World of Goods*, John Brewer and Roy Porter, eds., London, 1993.

5 Sidney Mintz, *Sweetness and Power*, London, 1985.

6 R.S.Dunn, *Sugar and Slaves. The Rise of the planter class in the English West Indies, 1624-1713*, London, 1973, p.203; Sidney Mintz, *op.cit.*, p.73.

7 K.N.Chaudhuri, *The Trading World of Asia and the East India Company*, Cambridge, 1978, pp.388-389.

8 Carole Shammas, *The Pre-Industrial Consumer in England and America*, Oxford, 1990, pp.83-85.

9 G.J.Barker-Benfield, *The Culture of Sensibility. Sex and Society in Eighteenth-Century Britain,* Chicago, 1992, pp.158-160.

10 Henry Hobhouse, *Seeds of Change*, London, 1985, pp.108-109.

11 N.McKendrick, 'Josiah Wedgwood and the commercialisation of the Potteries', in Neil McKendrick, John Brewer and J.H. Plumb, eds., *The Birth of a Consumer Society*, London, 1982.

12 Carole Shammas, 'Changes in English and Anglo-America Consumption from 1550-1800', in John Brewer and Roy Porter, eds., *op.cit.*, pp.181-185.

13 For the details, see Alan Kulikoff, *Tobacco and Slaves,* Chapel Hill, 1986.

14 Hoi-Cheung Mui and Lorna H. Mui, *Shops and Shopping in Eighteenth Century England,* London, 1989.

15 Cissie Fairchild, 'The Production and marketing of popluxe goods...', in John Brewer and Roy Porter, eds., *op.cit.*, pp.228-230.

16 Simon Schama, *Embarrassment of Riches*, London, 1987, p.206.

17 T.W. Devine, *The Tobacco Lords*, Edinburgh, 1990.

18 Dr Alexander Johnston, Notebook 1787(?), *Powel Papers*, Historical Society of Pennsylvania, Philadelphia; S.Pauli, *Treatise on Tobacco*, London, 1746, p.35.

19 J.R. Ward, *British West Indian Slavery, 1750-1834. The Process of Amelioration*, Oxford, 1988.

20 David Richardson, `Liverpool and the English Slave Trade', in *Transatlantic Slavery. Against Human Dignity,* Anthony Tibbles, ed., H.M.S.O., London, 1994, pp.71-73.

21 *Ibid,* p.75.

22 For examples of goods shipped from a small slaving port – Lancaster – (and their regional point of origin) see Melinda Elder, *The Slave Trade and the economic development of eighteenth century Lancaster,* Halifax, 1992, Appendix A, pp.211-212. For imports into a Jamaican plantation see Michael Craton and James Walvin, *op.cit.*, pp.320-327.

23 Nigel Tattersfield, *The Forgotten trade. Comprising the Log of the* Daniel and Henry *of 1700 and Accounts of the Slave Trade from the Minor Ports of England,1698-1725,* London, 1991.

24 David Richardson, *Liverpool, op.cit.*,p.75.

25 James Walvin, *England, Slaves and Freedom,* London, 1986; Seymour Drescher, *From Slavery, op.cit..*

26 Seymour Drescher, *From Slavery, op.cit..*

27 For the latest data see Herbet S. Klein, *The Atlantic Slave Trade*, Cambridge, 1999.

Chapter Three

1 James Walvin, *The Making of the Black Atlantic, op.cit.*

2 For the most recent – and best – account of slave life, see Philip D. Morgan, *Slave Counterpoint,* Chapel Hill, 1998.

3 Sidney Mintz, *op.cit...*

4 Robin Blackburn, *The Making of New World Slavery*, London, 1997.

5 Stuart Schwartz, *Sugar Plantations in the Formation of Brazilian Society. Bahia 1550-1835*, Cambridge, 1985.

6 Philip D. Curtin, *The Rise and Fall of the Plantation Complex*, Cambridge, 1990.

7 John Iliffe, *Africans. The History of a Continent,* Cambridge, 1995.

8 Hilary Beckles, *A History of Barbados*, Cambridge, 1990.

9 Johannes Menne Postmas, *The Dutch in the Atlantic Slave Trade, 1600-1815.* Cambridge, 1990.

10 See essays by David Richardson and Jacob Price, in P.J. Marshal, ed., *The Oxford History of the British Empire. The Eighteenth Century,* Oxford, 1998.

11 Michael Craton and James Walvin, *op.cit..*

12 James Walvin, *Fruits, op.cit.*, Ch.2.

13 John Brewer and Roy Porter, eds, *op.cit.*

14 Michael Symons, *One Continuous Picnic. A History of Eating in Australia,* Adelaide, 1982, p.16.

15 Roy Porter, *The Greatest Benefit to Mankind,* London, 1998.

16 Colin Campbell, *The Romantic Ethic and the Spirit of Modern Consumerism*, London, 1987

17 Jordan Goodman, *Tobacco in History*, London, 1993.

Chapter Four

1 For a good summary of the literature, see Richard Holt, *Sport and the British*, Oxford, 1989, Appendix, pp.357-367. But see also Peter Burke, *Sociology and History*, London, 1980. See also the brilliant essay by T. Judt, 'A clown in imperial purple', *History Workshop*, Spring 1979, pp.66-92.

2 For a useful survey, see Pat Hudson, *The Industrial Revolution*, London, 1992.

3 Charles Joyner, *Down by the Riverside*, Urbana, 1984, pp.131-131; Philip D. Morgan, *Slave Counterpoint*, Chapel Hill, 1998, pp.580-609; James Walvin, *Black Ivory. A History of British Slavery,* London, 1992, pp.157-164.

4 For a brilliant discussion see Michael A. Gomez, *Exchanging our Country Marks*, Chapel Hill, 1998.

5 The phrase is that of Mechal Sobel, *The World They Made Together*, Princeton, 1989.

6 *The Importance of Jamaica to Great Britain by a Gentleman*, London, 1744, pp.7-8.

7 Peter Burke, *Popular Culture in Early Modern Europe*, London, 1979; E.P. Thompson, *Customs in Common*, London, 1993.

8 Tweedie Estate Records, Jamaica Archives, February 1804, 4/45, No.40.

9 See essays in Ira Berlin and Philip D. Morgan, eds, *The Slave Economy*. Special Issue of *Slavery and Abolition*, Vol.12, No.1, May 1991.

10 *Slave Trials*, St Ann's, Jamaica, 29 August 1788 in M.S.273, National Library of Jamaica.

11 Bryan Edwards, *The History, Civil and Commercial of the West Indies,* 3rd edn, London, 1801, 3 vols, II, p.165.

12 *Ibid*, III, p.283.

13 Colin Campbell, *The Romantic Ethic and the Spirit of Modern Consumerism*, Oxford, 1987; James Axtell, 'The First Consumer Revolution', *Beyond 1492*, New York, 1992; John Brewer and Roy Porter, eds, *op.cit*.

14 B. Edwards, *op.cit*, III, p.250.

15 James Walvin, *Leisure and Society,* London, 1978, p.6.

16 J.R.Ward, *British West Indian Slavery, 1750-1834*, Oxford, 1988, pp.112-114.

17 See Law of 1770 in *The Laws of Jamaica*, St Jago, 1792, 2 vols, II, p.88.

18 For Europe, see Peter Burke, *Popular Culture, op. cit*. For Britain, see Richard Holt, *op.cit*.

19 J.R. Ward, *op. cit.*, p.114.

20 *An acccount of Jamaica and its Inhabitants, by a Gentleman*, London, 1808, p.262.

21 Frederick Douglass, *Narrative of the Life of Frederick Douglass, an American Slave*, Boston, 1845 edn, pp.75-76.

22 R.D. Abrahams and J.F. Szed, eds, *After Africa*, New Haven, 1983, especially chapters 3-6.

23 For a discussion of rational recreation see Richard Holt, *op. cit*, pp.136-148.

Chapter Five

1 Richard Dunn, *op.cit.*, pp.249-250.

2 P.L. Hughes and J.F. Larkin, eds, *Tudor Royal Proclamations*, New Haven, 1969, pp.221-222.

3 Baptisms of blacks in *Bedfordshire Parish Registers*, F.G. Emmison, ed: 1682 (vol.III); 1773 (vol.IV); 1766 vol.V); 1661 (Vol.VIII); 1710 (vol.X); 1735 (vol.XII); 1774 (vol.XIX); 1758 (vol.XXXIV); 1736/7 (vol.XXXVII).

4 1 October 1687, *Chamberlain's Accounts, 1680-1687*, Vol.27; 29 September 1687, *City of York, House Book, 1663-1688*, Vol.38. Both in City of York Archives.

5 *Yorkshire Archeological and Topographical Journal, 1879-1880*, Vol.VI, p.203 and p.393.

6 Norma Myers, *Reconstructing the Black Past. Blacks in Britain, 1780-1830*, London, 1996, pp.31-32 and 121-122.

7 *Interesting Narrative, op.cit.*, p.78.

8 Peter Fryer, *Staying Power*, London, 1984, pp.114-115.

9 Robin Blackburn, *The Making of New World Slavery. From the Baroque to the Modern, 1492-1800*, London, 1997.

10 We need to be alert to the distinction between 'British' and 'English' practice in these cases primarily because of the differences between English and Scottish law.

11 For the latest figures see Norma Myers, *op.cit.*

12 J.Ashton, *Social Life in the Reign of Queen Anne. Taken from Original Sources*, London, 1883, Detroit 1968 edn, p.63.

13 From *Tatler*, 1709. In *The Quarterly Review*, 1855, Vol.55, p.209.

14 *Ibid.*, p.210.

15 *Notes and Queries*, 1858, Vol.V, p.375.

16 *Ibid.,* Vol.VI, p.267.

17 *Liverpool and Slavery, by a Genuine "Dicky Sam"*, Liverpool, 1884, 1969 edn, p.9.

18 J.W. Damer Powell, *Bristol Privateers and Ships of War*, Bristol, 1930, p.126.

19 *Scot's Magazine*, 28, 1766, p.445.

20 *Notes and Queries*, 1852, Vol.VI, p.411.

21 Seymour Drescher, *Capitalism and Antislavery*, London, 1986, p.32.

22 Gretchen Gerzina, *Black England. Life before Emancipation*, London, 1996, p.7.

23 Reyahn King *et al*, eds, *Ignatius Sancho. An African Man of Letters*, London, 1997.

24 J. Ashton, *op.cit.*, pp.62-63.

25 For the latest account see Gretchen Gerzina, *op. cit.*

26 These cases are covered most recently in William R. Cotter, `The Somerset Case and the Abolition of Slavery in England,' *History*, vol.79, No.255, (1994) and William M. Wiecek, ` Somerset: Lord Mansfield and the Legitimacy of Slavery in the Anglo-American World,' *University of Chicago Law Review,* vol.42 (1974).

27 Gretchen Gerzina, *op. cit.*, p.130.

28 *Scot's Magazine*, 36, 1774, p.53.

29 *Horace Walpole Correspondence*, W.S. Lewis *et al*, eds, Oxford, 1966, vol.31, pp.340 and 350.

30 See the story of the black lover press-ganged because of his love affair with a married white woman, *The Times*, 11-12 February, 1794.

31 `The Slave Grace, 1827', H.T. Catterall, *Judicial Cases concerning American Slavery and the Negro*, Washington, 5 vols., 1926-36, Vol.I, pp.34-37.

Chapter Six

1 For a recent contribution to this discussion see J. R. Oldfield, *Popular Politics and British Anti-Slavery*, Manchester, 1995.

2 Linda Colley, *Britons. Forging the Nation, 1707-1837*, London, 1992, pp.142-143.

3 J. R. Oldfield, *op. cit.*, p.33.

4 *Ibid.*, Chapter 4.

5 The best books on Haiti are David Geggus, *Slavery, War and Revolution*, Oxford, 1982 and Robin Blackburn, *The Overthrow of Colonial* Slavery, London, 1988. The classic account by C.L.R. James, *Black Jacobins*, though now dated in its detail, remains essential reading for any student of the Haitian revolt.

Chapter Seven

1 Clive Emsley, *British Society and the French Wars*, London, 1979.

2 Quoted in Linda Colley, *Britons*, New Haven, 1992, p.359.

3 David Eltis, *Economic Growth and the Ending of the Transatlantic Slave Trade*, Oxford, 1987, Ch.2.

4 See essays in Patrick O'Brien and Roland Quinault, eds, *The Industrial Revolution and British Society*, Cambridge, 1993; Seymour Drescher, *From Slavery*, op.cit.

5 See essays in P.J. Marshall, ed., *Oxford History of the British Empire. The Eighteenth Century*, Oxford, 1998.

6 Seymour Drescher, *Capitalism and Antislavery*, London, 1987.

7 Bernard Porter, *The Lion's Share: A Short History of British Imperialism*, London, 1975, pp.39-40.

8 Elizabeth Savage, ed., *The Human Commodity. Perspectives on the Trans-Saharan Slave Trade*, London, 1992.

9 Raymond C. Howell, *The Royal Navy and the Slave Trade*, London, 1987, p.209.

10 See essays in John M. MacKenzie, ed., *Imperialism and Popular Culture*, Manchester, 1986.

11 Linda Colley, *Britons*, op. cit., p.359.

12 *Ibid.*, p.361.

13 Quoted in James Walvin, *Black Ivory. A History of British Slavery*, London, 1992, p.309

14 Linda Colley, *Britons*, op.cit., p.360.

15 See essays in E.J. Hobsbawm and T. Ranger, eds, *The Invention of Tradition*, Cambridge, 1983.

16 Alexandria Scott, ed., *Musica Britannica*, London, 1981; J.J. Fudd, *The Book of World Famous Music*, New York, 1966, p.477; J.N. Ander-Bach, ed., *The*

Catalogue of Printed Music in the British Library to 1980, vol.2, London, 1981, pp.148-151.

17 Linda Colley, *Britons, op.cit.*, p.260.

Chapter Eight

1 James Walvin, *An African 's Life. The Life and Times of Olaudah Equiano*, London, 1998; Vincent Carretta, ed., *The Interesting Narrative of Olaudah Equiano* (1789), London, 1995.

2 *York Herald*, 21 April 1792

3 *The Gentleman's Magazine*, April 1797, pp.67 and 356.

4 *The Interesting Narrative*, Belper, 1809, p. vi. British Library copy.

5 *A tribute for the Negro being a Vindication of the Moral, Intellectual, and Religious Capabilities of the Coloured portion of mankind…*, Manchester, 1848, pp.192-239.

6 William Armistead, *A cloud of Witness against Slavery and Oppression*, London, 1853; H. G. Adams, ed., *God's Image in Ebony*, London, 1854.

7 Paul Edwards, ed., *Equiano's Travels*, London, 1967; P.D. Curtin, ed., *Africa Remembered*, Madison, Wisconsin, 1967.

8 For the best recent anthology see Vincent Carretta, ed., *Unchained Voices*, Lexington, 1996.

9 *The Letters of the Late Ignatius Sancho*, Paul Edwards, ed., London, 1968; Reyahn King *et al, op.cit.*

10 Norma Myers, *Reconstructing the Black Past. Blacks in Britain, 1870-1830*, London, 1996.

11 *Ibid.*

12 In James Walvin, *An African's Life, op. cit.*, Ch.4.

13 *Unchained Voices,* op. cit., p. 184, n. 63.

14 *Ibid.*, p.11.

15 Letter, 27 February 1792, in *The Interesting Narrative...*, *op. cit.*, p.346.

16 Thomas Clarkson, *The History of the Rise, Progress and Accomplishment of the Abolition of the Slave Trade*, London, 1808, 2 vols, I, pp.85-125.

17 James Walvin, *Black and White. The Negro and English Society, 1555-1945*, London, 1973; F.O. Shyllon, *Black Slaves in Britain*, Oxford, 1974; F.O. Shyllon, *Black People in Britain, 1555-1833*, Oxford, 1977; Peter Fryer, *Staying Power*, London, 1984.

Chapter Ten

1 See Introduction, *Letters of the Late Ignatius Sancho, An African*, (1782), Vincent Carretta, ed., London, 1998 edn.

Chapter Eleven

1 *Interesting Narrative*, *op.cit.*, pp.232-235.

2 See the essays in Mark Philp, ed., *The French Revolution and British Popular Politics*, Cambridge, 1991.

3 For recent studies of early abolition see J.R. Oldfield, *Popular Politics and British Anti-Slavery. The mobilisation of public opinion against the slave trade, 1787-1807*, Manchester, 1995; Judith Jennings, *The Business of Abolishing the British Slave Trade, 1783-1807*, London, 1997.

4 Judith Jennings, *op.cit.*; James Walvin, *The Quakers. Money and Morals*, London, 1997, Ch.5.

5 James Walvin, *The Quakers*, *op.cit.*, pp.126-128.

6 John Kemp, *Commonplace book*, 1786, MS Box X3/2, Library of the Friends Meeting House, Euston Road, London.

7 Thomas Clarkson, *op.cit.*, vol.I. pp.85-125.

8 Roger Anstey, *The Atlantic Slave Trade and British Abolition, 1760-1810*, London, 1975,.pp.276-7.

9 But see discussion of slavery in the following radical tracts: John Butler, *Brief Reflections Upon the Liberty of the British Subject*, Canterbury, 1792; Henry York, *Reason Urged Against Precedence. In a Letter to the People of Derby*, 1793; D.I.Eaton, *Extermination or An Appeal to the People of England on the Present War with France*, London ,1793.

10 See Michael Duffy, 'War,revolution and the crisis of the British Empire', in Mark Philp, *op. cit.*, p.118.

11 Michael Duffy, 'World-Wide War and British Expansion,1793-1815', in P.J.Marshall, ed., *The Oxford History of the British Empire. The Eighteenth Century*, Oxford, 1998, Ch.9.

12 David Geggus, `Slavery, War and Revolution in the Greater Caribbean, 1789-1815', in David Barry Gaspar and David Patrick Geggus, eds., *A Turbulent Time in the Caribbean. The French Revolution and the Greater Caribbean*, Bloomington and Indianapolis, 1997.

13 Michael Duffy, `British Attitudes to the West Indian Colonies', *ibid.*, pp.88-89.

14 Norma Myers, *op.cit.*, Ch.2.

15 David Dabydeen, *Hogarth's Blacks*, London, 1985.

16 *Isaac Cruikshank and the Politics of Parody*, Huntington Library, 1994, pp.41 and 71.

17 See incident reported in *The Times*, 11-12 February 1794.

18 James Walvin, *Equiano, op.cit.*, Ch.13.

19 See entry for 19 March, 1783, Granville Sharp, *Diary,1783-1798*,Gloucester Record Office.

20 W. Jeffrey Bolster, *Black Jacks. African American Seamen in the Age of Sail*, Cambridge MA, 1997.

21 *Interesting Narrative, op.cit.*, pp.233-235.

22 James Walvin, *Questioning Slavery*, London, 1996, Ch.8.

Chapter Twelve

1 It plays little role in R.R. Palmer, *The Age of Democratic Revolution,* 2 vols., Princeton, 1958.

2 David Geggus, *Slavery,War and Revolution,* Oxford, 1982; David Barry Gaspar and David Patrick Geggus, eds., *op. cit.*

3 James Walvin, *Fruits of Empire, op.cit.*

4 Robin Blackburn, *The Making of New World Slavery, op.cit.*, Ch.1.

5 James Walvin, *Equiano, op. cit.*, p.51, n.28-31.

6 David Brion Davis, *The Problem of Slavery in Western Culture*, Ithaca, 1966.

Index